triathlon
training
cycling

Lynda Wallenfels

triathlon
training

cycling

Published in 2005 by
A&C Black Publishers Ltd
37 Soho Square, London W1D 3QZ
www.acblack.com

Published in the United States of America in 2005 as
The Triathlete's Guide to Bike Training by
VeloPress®
1830 North 55th Street
Boulder, Colorado 80301–2700 USA
303/440-0601 • Fax 303/444-6788 • E-mail velopress@insideinc.com

ISBN 0 7136 7459 8

A CIP catalogue number for this book is available from the British Library.

*Before embarking on any strenuous exercise program, including the
training described in this book, everyone, particularly anyone with a
known heart or blood pressure problem, should be examined by a
pysician.*

Cover image © Getty Images/ Karl Weatherly

Cover design by James Watson
Interior design and composition by Rebecca Finkel, F + P Graphic Design, Inc.
Photo 2.1 (page 18) by Cameron Elford. Photo 4.1 (page 67) by Quinn Pratt.
All other photos were provided by the author.

Printed in the United States of America

To Steve —

Thanks for giving me the space and

encouragement to do what I love.

Contents

Foreword

In late 1994, Lynda Wallenfels called me. At the time, she was a professional mountain bike racer and was looking for a coach for the coming season. I was on her list of coaches to interview for the job partly because we both lived in Ft. Collins, Colorado.

I had never been through a more detailed questioning by an athlete. Most just asked if I'd coach them. That wasn't Lynda's style. She was well prepared with a long list of questions and obviously knew exactly what she was looking for in a coach. As I recall, the telephone interview lasted nearly an hour with the questions ranging from administrative matters (How often would we talk?) to philosophical issues (Are there differences in how you coach men and women?).

When we finished the interview, I figured I was out of the running, since she never indicated agreement with what I was saying—just an occasional "Uh-huh." I was wrong. A few days later Lynda called to see if we could meet.

Lynda and I worked together for about four years, during which time she proved to be an athlete to reckon with on the tough NORBA (National Off-Road Bicycling Association) circuit and twice won the Scottish National Mountain Bike Championship (she's a Scottish citizen).

She also proved to be a very intelligent athlete who always wanted to understand why I had written the schedule as I had. Superficial answers weren't good enough; she always wanted to know the "bottom-line" explanation. I could tell early on that she had many traits found in good coaches—an inquisitive mind, a passion for detail, an excellent understanding of human physiology, a strong interest in helping others, and a great love for the sport.

After she retired from pro racing in 1998 and moved to St. George, Utah, I figured I would seldom see her again. But in May 2001, Lynda emailed me to say she had taken up triathlon and was coaching. She also asked if my company, Ultrafit Associates, would consider accepting her as one of our coaching associates. I explained our tough application process, but down deep I knew she'd be approved.

Now the tables were reversed—I got to put *her* through the grinder. Since membership approval is done by our Board of Advisors, made up of current associates who are highly concerned with the quality of the coaches we bring onboard, the process for approval is demanding. Lynda passed with flying colors, and in October 2001, she officially became one of our associates.

Lynda has proven to be an exceptional coach. When I began to think about producing an Ultrafit Multisport Training Series, she was an obvious choice for the cycling book. I was pleased when she accepted the challenge. Having read the manuscript, I know that I made the right decision.

As you read this book, you'll come to understand what has made Lynda Wallenfels a master coach. Your knowledge of the bike leg of multisport racing will also grow, making you a better athlete.

JOE FRIEL
ULTRAFIT TRAINING SERIES EDITOR

Acknowledgments

I would like to thank Joe Friel for bringing me under his wing as an athlete, guiding my way while I was racing, and encouraging me to pursue a coaching career. My thanks also goes to each and every member coach of Ultrafit Associates for allowing me to draw daily on their huge base of collective knowledge, for educating me, and for helping me better serve my athletes. Special thanks to Ken Mierke, who read the manuscript and provided valuable technical input, and to Gordo Byrn, who was always happy to discuss training and share his experience.

I am grateful to my parents for teaching me to ride a bike not long after I could walk and for making sure I always had a bike to ride no matter my age or size; to my husband, Steve Wallenfels, for providing me support on every level and encouraging me to pursue that which makes me happy; and to my athletes for keeping me thinking, having faith in me, and following my training ideas and programs.

Thanks to all the following people who contributed to the completion of this book: Carmella Livorsi at Specialized Bikes, Mike Hanseen at Canyon Bicycles in Salt Lake City, Jen Todd, Quinn Pratt, and the editors at VeloPress.

Preface

The popularity of the sport of triathlon is skyrocketing worldwide. With increased race participation, the level and depth of competition for all age groups is increasing rapidly. Athletes with years of experience in the sport can no longer be complacent about their training if they want to win; newcomers are chasing them down. Triathletes need to step up their game each year to remain at the top.

CYCLING IS THE MOST TECHNICAL DISCIPLINE

The conventional wisdom circulated in the subculture of triathlon is that swimming requires the most skill, followed by running, and cycling—the least technical of all. As the urban legend goes, all you have to do to be a good cyclist is ride a lot. If you are an athlete looking to win, you should encourage all of your competitors to adhere to this theory, and then look closely at reality yourself.

When viewed from the narrow aspect of the single repetitive action each sport requires, cycling is less technical. One swim stroke requires you to keep your body in perfect balance in the water, enter your hand in just the right place, catch a full arm of water, and move yourself forward through this slippery medium. One run step requires you to be vertically balanced, coordinate the movement of your arms and legs, strike the ground with the correct part of your foot, and spring forward without springing up too much. In contrast, on the bike your feet are fixed in place on the pedals, and the pattern of movement is fixed by the crank-arm revolution. One single pedal stroke is indeed less technical than one run stride or one swim stroke.

However, we can also view each sport from a broader perspective. When swimming, you are always in water (obviously). The terrain does not change much. Racecourses are always flat with few turns, water density remains constant, and your swim speed does not change significantly. You may encounter waves, currents, and varying temperatures in open water, but in general, swimming conditions are very constant. The challenge of adapting to different bodies of water is minimal.

Environmental conditions on the run can vary dramatically—flats, hills, wind, rain, corners—and in off-road events anything is possible, including rocks, sand, creeks, and mud. However, your running speed does not change dramatically despite varying conditions, and your stride pattern stays relatively consistent.

When cycling, you encounter all of the same environmental conditions as running; however, you're often traveling at much greater speeds, balancing on top a chunk of metal with rotating wheels, and your contact with the ground is two very small patches of rubber. Tell me cycling does not take more skill than running or swimming!

Because of the nature of cycling, the opportunities for gaining "free speed" with improved cycling skills arc HUGE. Developing your ability to stay in an aero position and flow around a fast corner can save you five seconds or more over an athlete of equal fitness who sits up and hangs onto the brakes through the turn. Coasting down a 1-mile descent at 40 mph will gain you 30 seconds over a competitor of equal fitness who only has the skill to descend at 30 mph. Would 30 seconds affect your overall placing? A skilled rider may rest and stretch during a 40-mph descent, whereas an unskilled rider may be gripping the handlebars, rigid with fear, at 30 mph. The unskilled rider may need a rest after the hill and lose even more time.

Riding a lot is at the heart of bike training, but what you do with your time on the bike will dictate your development and progression as a cyclist. To put down the fastest bike split in a race, you need to have a quiver full of abilities: handling skills to speed in and out of the transition area, speed through corners and over hills, an efficient pedal stroke, an aerodynamic bike setup, a comfortable and powerful position, and the ability to manipulate your cadence and manage your energy expenditure to ensure a solid run split. Train hard to develop a high level of fitness, but also train *smart* to build a full range of cycling skills. Skilled and fit cyclists will finish in front of fit cyclists every time.

This book is a practical guide designed to educate and lead you through your development as a cyclist. Part One covers equipment selection and bike setup specific to your chosen event. Part Two focuses on riding skills and pedaling techniques, training principles, and heart rate and power training modalities. Part Three leads you step-by-step through the process of designing a custom training plan based on your unique abilities and race schedule. Part Four contains training plans for sprint-distance, off-road, half-ironman–distance, and full ironman–distance triathlons. Each of the four plans was designed using the training principles established throughout the book. At the end, you will find a full menu of cycling training sessions, categorized by ability, to help you structure your training week.

PART ONE

Bike Setup

C H A P T E R

1 Equipment

Triathlon is an equipment-intensive sport. To compete, you need to have gear for swimming, biking, and running (which adds up to a carload), and there are many added extras that are nice to have during training. Although the fitness and strength of a rider are the biggest determining factors in performance, equipment is a key area where improvements can be made. Obviously, you will go faster with less energy on a 19-pound, titanium, triathlon filly than a 40-pound, discount-store steed. A fast bike will make any rider, regardless of his or her level, faster. Energy-wise, equipment improvements are free speed. Dollar-wise, however, they can be very costly.

On average, the power produced to pedal a bike along a flat road is spent as 60% rider drag, 12% rolling resistance, 8% wheel drag, 8% frame drag, 8% bike/rider inertia, 0.5% wheel inertia, and 3.5% miscellaneous forces. While the area in which you can achieve the biggest performance gains is rider drag, every little bit helps. This chapter will help you select the best, most efficient equipment for your cycling needs.

HELMETS

Helmet companies have produced a lot of nice data demonstrating that helmets do not make your head heat up and that a helmet is more aerodynamic than your bare head. The bottom line, however, is safety—helmets save lives. Everybody, including me, has a story about a crash that has ended with a helmet split in two. So get a good helmet and wear it every minute you are on the bike.

Be sure that your helmet has been approved for cycling by the Consumer Product Safety Commission (CPSC) and that it fits properly. A helmet does not work if it rolls off your head during a crash. Cycling helmets are designed to be crushed (rather than your skull) on impact, and once they are crushed you need to replace them. Frequently check the condition of your helmet; a new one is vastly cheaper than a trip to the emergency room.

THE BIKE

There is a dizzying array of bikes available, made from different materials, built with different geometries, and optimized for different purposes. To determine the type of bike that is best for you, consider the primary event in which you will compete. Short course or long course? On road or off road? You want the fastest machine to handle the job you are giving it. Weight, handling ability, aerodynamics, and comfort will all factor into your decision. In shorter events, weight and aerodynamics are most important, and a degree of comfort can be sacrificed for speed. In longer events such as the ironman, comfort becomes paramount to continued optimal performance over long periods of time. The slower speeds and rougher terrain of off-road events make agility, handling ease, and the weight of the bike more important than aerodynamics.

When looking for a new bike, you have a lot of choices. The best way to find the bike that fits your needs, abilities, and body type is to consult with a qualified bike fit professional. A bike fit expert will measure you and help you research the best bikes that are both in your price range and suit your needs. (See Chapter 2 to determine the perfect machine for you.)

FRAME
Materials

The frame material defines the weight, strength, stiffness, durability, and cost of a bike. Most frames are constructed of steel, aluminum, titanium, or carbon fiber. Each metal has unique characteristics around which the frames are designed. For example, aluminum frames have large-diameter tubes with thin walls compared to steel frames.

Steel is cheap and easy to work with, thus it can produce the least expensive frames. Compared to the other frame materials, it is heavy, but improved steel frames with Reynolds 831, Dedacciai, or Columbus tubing can rival the lightest frames built from other materials. A well-made steel frame will last many years with proper care, but steel can rust, which is a major drawback in humid climates.

Aluminum is reasonably priced, lightweight, rustproof, stiff, and responsive, and aluminum tubes can be easily and cost-effectively formed into aerodynamic shapes. An aluminum frame can be too stiff and uncomfortable on long rides, however. It is difficult to repair and only has a life expectancy of about five years.

Titanium is smooth, supple, light, responsive, rustproof, and absorbs road shock for a comfortable ride. It is half as dense as steel and makes the lightest frames available. A titanium frame is very durable and will last forever. It is the most expensive of the frame materials, however, and is difficult to repair.

Carbon Fiber is four-times stronger than high-tensile steel for the same weight. It can be molded into any shape, and its fibers are oriented to make it stiffer laterally than vertically. This means a carbon fiber frame will not flex with hard pedaling but will still absorb road shock. Carbon fiber is rustproof, but it can be difficult to repair and is usually expensive.

Geometry

Frame geometry is determined by the length of the tubes and the angles at which they intersect. The geometry of a bike dictates how it will handle, steer, and perform. The most common frame geometry is the double diamond shape (see Photo 1.1). The front triangle is comprised of the top tube (A), seat tube (B), and down tube (C). The rear triangle is comprised of the seat tube (B), seat stays (D), and chain stays (E). Several alternative frame designs are available. The Kestrel KM40 Airfoil looks like a double diamond design but is missing the seat tube (see Photo 1.2). Softride beam bikes have a unique design with a shock-absorbing beam, on which the rider sits, extending out from the head tube.

PHOTO 1.1 *Standard double diamond frame design*

PHOTO 1.2 *The Kestrel KM40 is a carbon fiber bike with no seat tube.*

Seat-tube angle is calculated as the degrees the seat tube deviates from horizontal. A seat-tube angle of 80 degrees sits relatively upright and is referred to as "steep" or "aggressive." A seat-tube angle of 73 degrees is more laid back and is referred to as "slack." A steep seat tube puts the rider forward on the bike into an aggressive, aerodynamic position. A slack seat tube puts a rider farther back on the bike, making it handle in a more stable and agile manner.

COMPONENTS
Gears

In order to select the correct gears for your bike, an understanding of gearing is necessary. Bikes come with two or three front chainrings and eight, nine, or ten cogs on the rear hub. When gearing is written in shorthand, the front chainring is listed first, followed by a slash and then the rear cog. For example, a gear that uses the 53-tooth chain- ring and 12-tooth cog will be written as 53/12. (Experienced cyclists are familiar with the effort required to ride this gear, and 53/12 is a meaningful term to them.) The largest and smallest chain rings and cogs would be described as 53/39 and 12-23. Other methods used to describe the gears on a bike are gear development and gear inches.

Gear development, measured in feet, is the distance the bike travels in one pedal revolution. Changing the combination of chainrings and cogs will change the gear development. Gear development charts can be consulted to compare gear development figures for every gear combination. For example a 53/19 has a gear development of 19.3 feet.

Gear inches is a ratio comparing gears determined by dividing the number of teeth on the chainring by the number of teeth on the cog, then multiplying the result by the diameter of the wheel in inches. For example, a 39-tooth chainring and a 25-tooth cog on a 27-inch wheel (700c) would be:

(39 ÷ 25) x 27 = 42.12

Gearing semantics are related to gear development. A 42/19 combination has a gear development of 15.3, and a 53/13 combination has a gear development of 28.25. We say the 53/13 is a "bigger" gear than the 42/19. Shifting up a gear refers to increasing the gear development and the load. (You shift "up" to a bigger gear and "down" to a smaller gear.) The confusing part is that, visually, the size of the cogs do not match the above descriptions but are reversed. When you move the chain to a smaller cog your chain moves down the cogs, but you are shifting up and selecting a bigger gear.

When determining what gears to put on your bike, first decide the largest and smallest gears you need; the gaps in between can subsequently be filled. To set up your bike to train in hilly terrain or for a hilly race, you should increase the size of your biggest cog. This will give you a smaller (easier) gear for pedaling uphill. Also consider your abilities. A rider who prefers to pedal at a fast cadence should select a smaller gear combination than a rider who prefers a slower cadence.

The most commonly used gears are:

- 700c wheels 53/39 and 12-23
- 650c wheels 55/42 and 12-23
- 26" mountain bike wheels 24/34/46 and 12-32

Pedals

When selecting a pedal model to use, you should consider the amount of float and stability you require. The degree of float on most pedals is adjustable. As the degree of float increases, the amount of stability the pedal provides the ankle and knee decreases. Athletes with stability issues, such as weak hip and knee stabilizing muscles, should choose a pedal with a larger platform and less float to keep the legs stable and in correct alignment throughout the pedal stroke.

Wheels

The two dominant factors affecting wheel performance are weight and aerodynamics. There is not one particular wheel on the market that is "the fastest," as this distinction also depends upon the course profile and the wind conditions. On flat, straight courses, aerodynamics are more important than weight. On hilly courses, or ones with many turns requiring frequent accelerations, wheel weight becomes increasingly important over aerodynamics. It is more difficult and requires more energy to accelerate a heavy wheel up to speed, but once at speed, the aerodynamics of the wheel determine its performance. You must analyze your goal racecourse and decide the optimal setup for you. If your race is hilly, go for a light-weight wheel set. If your race is straight and flat, go for an aerodynamic set.

Wheel aerodynamics

Rim depth and shape are the most important aspects of aerodynamic wheel design, followed by spoke count, shape, and diameter, and hub shape. As rims deepen, wheel surface area increases and aerodynamics improve. However, deep rims make the bike difficult to handle in cross-winds. This will drain your energy and slow your times. If your goal race has a reputation for being windy, such as Ironman® Hawaii, deep rims and full discs may cause stability problems. Fewer spokes equal better aerodynamics.

Wheel size

It is difficult to compare 650c wheels to 700c wheels, as there are pros and cons for both. Again, you must analyze your goal event and your personal characteristics to decide which size is best for you. Riders who are less than 5'4" should select a 650c wheel size for a number of reasons. Once a head tube and handlebars have been stacked over a 700c wheel on a small frame, the front end of the bike will be too high for the rider to achieve a low, aerodynamic position. The smaller wheel size will also reduce the risk of toe overlap common on small frames with 700c wheels. Toe overlap occurs during pedaling when the toe touches the front wheel while it is being turned—obviously an undesirable and crash-causing situation. Most 650c wheels are lighter than 700c wheels, thus riders entered into very hilly events will also do better with the smaller size. However, a 700c wheel has more surface area than a 650c wheel and is more aerodynamic when rotating. Riders in events with flat courses will be more aerodynamic with 700c wheels provided they can achieve an aerodynamic body position on the bike. Thus, riders taller than 5'9" will usually benefit from a 700c wheel.

Tires

The tires are the points at which your bike touches the ground. The tread pattern, width, design, and inflation pressure define the rolling resistance and traction your bike will have. It is important to select tires that will maximize your performance and confidence.

Tubulars versus clinchers

Tubular tires do not have an inner tube and use glue to hold them in place on the rim. Clincher tires do need an inner tube. Clinchers have a bead that hooks onto the rim to hold them in place. Tubulars plus rims generally weigh less than clincher/tube/rim combinations and can be inflated to higher pressures, which reduces rolling resistance. However, if your rims or tires have been previously glued and are not meticulously cleaned of glue residue before remounting, there is no rolling resistance or weight advantage to tubulars. Tubulars are more expensive, more difficult to repair, and spares are bulky to carry, but tubulars are more resistant to punctures than clinchers, and in the event of a flat tire they are very quick to change. To fix clinchers, you have to extract and either patch or replace the inner tube. This can be time consuming, but it eliminates the need to carry a spare tire.

Tread patterns for off-road tires

Full-tread tires come in many shapes and sizes. Some tires are designed for specific conditions, but the biggest deciding factor in tire selection is personal preference; ride a few different tread patterns to see what you like. Semi-slick tires have a bald or very low-tread center and aggressive knobbies on the sides. The bald center greatly reduces rolling resistance over a full-tread tire and makes for a much faster ride. No knobbies also means less cushioning, a harsher ride, and an increased likelihood of a pinch flat, however.

Most off-road triathlon courses are relatively non-technical, and a rider with excellent bike-handling abilities will gain a significant advantage by riding with semi-slicks. These tires generally corner, climb, and descend well on hard-packed terrain. Semi-slicks are also faster in sticky mud, as full-tread tires carry more mud between the knobbies and get weighed down. But when the conditions become loose, gravelly, or very wet, semi-slicks provide poor traction. They will also lose traction on extremely steep terrain and with hard braking. These problems can be minimized with skillful riding, however, so if you have the skill and confidence to ride them, semi-slicks are the fastest option.

Tire pressure

Choosing the correct tire pressure can make or break a race. Keep the following points in mind when deciding your air pressure:

- Higher tire pressure minimizes rolling resistance, but it gives a harsher ride and reduces traction.

- Lower tire pressure increases the risk of pinch flats.

- A heavier rider will need a higher tire pressure than a lighter rider.

- Rear wheels carry more rider weight than front wheels and should be inflated 10-percent higher.

- Tubular tires can be inflated to higher pressures than clinchers.

- The maximum recommended tire pressure will be written on the side of the tire.

Hydration Systems

There are numerous choices for hydration systems. You can choose from standard frame-mounted water bottles, water bottles mounted behind the seat, an aero-shaped bottle with a sipping straw between the aerobars, a hydration backpack, and a pressurized pouch slung beneath the seat with a sipping straw extended to the handlebars. The aerodynamic cost of each system depends on how often you will be drinking. The bottles hidden behind the seat are aerodynamic when they are not in use, but grabbing them and drinking causes drag. Overall, a hydration backpack has been shown to create the least drag when both carrying and drinking are taken into consideration. The aerobar bottle is the next best option. Due to the importance of staying fueled and hydrated in longer events, the bottom line is that the best hydration system is the one you like and will use efficiently and continually.

Shoes

Triathletes should race in cycling-specific shoes, which have stiffer soles than running shoes. A stiff sole directly transfers power to the pedals—power that can be lost with soft soles. Cycling shoes also reduce hot spots and foot numbness that can be caused by the pedal platform pressing against a small area of the foot. Speed of entry and exit into and out of the shoe is an important consideration for speedy transitions. Shoes that fasten with Velcro straps are faster to change in transitions than shoes with laces.

TRAINING MONITORS
Heart Rate Monitors

Heart rate monitors (HRMs) measure beats per minute (bpm). A transmitter picks up the heartbeat and sends a signal to a wristwatch or handlebar-mounted computer. There is a vast selection of heart rate monitors available, and models vary in price from $50 to more than $300 depending on the bells and whistles they offer. At a minimum, purchase a model that will calculate your average heart rate over the duration and during a portion of a workout.

PHOTO 1.3 *Polar heart rate monitor*

Power Meters

Though scientific studies have been measuring on-bike power output in terms of wattage for decades, on-bike power meters have only recently become available to the cycling community at large. A power meter provides objective and immediate feedback on the amount of work being done and the intensity of the exercise. The three most common on-bike power meters are the SRM (Schoberer Rad Messtechnik), Power-Tap, and Polar S-710. Power output can also be recorded while riding on stationary trainers such as the CompuTrainer, Tacx Ergotrainer, and Velotron. However, these power trainers are not as versatile as on-bike power meters that can be used when riding on the open road.

The SRM uses strain gauges in the crank to measure torque and pedaling cadence to measure angular velocity. The product of these two components yields power. To set up an SRM on your bike, you need to replace the cranks and mount a chain-stay receiver, a fork speed sensor, and the handlebar computer-processing unit (CPU). Using this system on multiple bikes is moderately time consuming, as it requires transferring all of these components from one bike to another. SRMs are available in three models—the Amateur, the Professional, and the Science—with reported accuracies of +/- 5%, +/- 2%, and +/- 0.5% respectively. SRMs are the most expensive of the power meters, with the Amateur retailing for $1,800, the Professional for $2,600, and the Science for $4,600.

The Power-Tap uses strain gauges in the rear hub to measure torque and simultaneously track the hub's angular velocity in order to calculate power. The Power-Tap is the easiest power meter to install. Simply put a cassette and tire on the Power-Tap wheel, put the wheel on your bike, zip-tie a receiver on the seat stays, and mount the computer-processing unit on your handlebars. The Power-Tap is easy to transfer between multiple bikes. If the second bike has the receiver and CPU mount (harness), all you need to do is switch the rear wheel. Two Power-Tap models are available; the Pro model retails for $899

PHOTO 1.4 *Power-Tap hub and CPU*

and the Standard model sells for $699. The reported accuracy for the Standard model is +/- 1.5 percent.

The Polar S-710 uses a chain-frequency sensor, a chain-speed sensor, a speed sensor, and cadence sensors to determine power. These four sensors need to be in exactly the right places in order to work properly, which can make the system finicky to set up and difficult to transfer between multiple bikes. The Polar S-710 model with power meter option retails for $650.

A Word About Safety

During bike racing and training, you reach far greater speeds than in swimming or running, and you often share the road with motor vehicles. These two elements can be a deadly combination, so you must take care to minimize your risk of an accident. Again, always wear your helmet, even on short, low-speed jaunts. These casual rides are often where crashes occur, and it's important to pay as much attention when you are riding at a relaxed 10 mph as when you are hammering at 40 mph.

Check your bike before every ride. Inspect the tires for thorns or wear spots, check to be sure that your brakes contact the rims, not the tires, and ensure that all bolts are tight. Wear sunscreen, sunglasses, and gloves to protect yourself from the elements, and always check to be sure that your helmet is securely fastened before you head out on your bike.

Road rage

Follow the traffic rules when you ride. Be particularly aware of motorists pulling out of sideroads. Bikes are often overlooked, as drivers are more aware of other cars. Be courteous to motorists in all situations. For the safety of other cyclists, report the license plates of motorists who violate traffic rules to the authorities. Car-to-bike road rage is not uncommon. When a confrontation between a car and a bicycle occurs, the cyclist always comes off worse—sometime fatally so. It doesn't matter who is right or wrong when your safety is at stake.

CHAPTER

2 Position Setup

Bike fit is crucial to your performance, comfort, and happiness on the bike. A proper fit is the key to being an efficient cyclist, and it will make a big difference in your race times. Efficiency is expressed as the ratio of work done to energy expended; being efficient means getting the most speed from the energy you put into the pedals. Additionally, a proper fit will enhance stability, allowing you to control your bike at high speeds. Simply put, you will never be your best on a poorly fit bike.

BIKE FIT VERSUS BIKE POSITION

Bike fit and bike position are two different things. Bike fit involves the selection of equipment, such as frame, handlebars, and crank, which, when put together, makes a bike that is the correct size for you. Unfortunately there is not a formula or recipe you can follow to get the perfect bike fit. According to Dr. Andy Pruitt from the Boulder Center for Sports Medicine in Boulder, Colorado, no single, generic position is suitable for all triathletes. "The bike needs to look like you. It must resemble your anatomy," says Pruitt. Ken Mierke, an Ultrafit coach, adds "I like to tell athletes that we need to adapt the bike to them, not their bodies to the bike. This is especially important for riders whose bodies lack perfect symmetry. If your body is not symmetrical, your bike definitely should not be either."

Bike position involves setting the adjustable parts of the bike to optimize your posture on the bike. You can be in a casual "sit up and beg" position or hunched down in an aggressive, aerodynamic position. Your body's position on the bike affects how efficiently you will ride and how fast you will be able to go. An optimal position is one in which you analyze your goals, body type, and abilities, and set your position accordingly. Therefore, a recreational cyclist will have a very different position than a world champion racer.

POWER VERSUS AERODYNAMICS VERSUS COMFORT

Body position on the bike influences your power, aerodynamics, and comfort. An optimal position for triathlon racing is a comfortable, aerodynamic position in which you can produce the most power and have the most efficient pedal stroke. There is generally a trade-off between these factors. The most comfortable position, the most aerodynamic position, the position in which you can produce the highest power output, and the position in which you can pedal most efficiently will rarely be the same. The trade-offs made between each are based on your goals, body type, abilities, and the duration and terrain of your priority races. A sprint-distance specialist can accept a less-comfortable position in order to gain power and aerodynamic benefits. As the duration of a ride increases, the importance of comfort increases. An ironman-distance racer must place a higher emphasis on comfort, as this rider needs to be comfortable for five-plus hours on the bike. Any speed benefit gained by improved aerodynamics will be completely negated when an uncomfortable bike forces an athlete to pull over to stretch, rest, or quit the race altogether.

The most aerodynamic position is almost always inferior in terms of power generation, and trading some aero for a more-powerful position usually pays off. Some of the top cyclists ride very quickly and efficiently in a position that is not particularly aerodynamic. Powerful athletes should be positioned on their bikes to take full advantage of their strength, while less-powerful riders may be faster in a more aerodynamic position. At this point you encounter the "art" of bike setup. Unless you have access to wind-tunnel testing, you will be guessing about the aerodynamics, but this chapter will provide you with some guidelines so you can make an educated guess.

Aerodynamics are crucial at all speeds—not just fast ones. Drag increases exponentially with speed, thus, when going fast, riders have more to gain by improving their aerodynamics than when they are riding slowly. At 12 mph about half of the work done on a bike is to overcome air resistance. At 25 mph more than 80 percent of the work being done is needed to overcome air resistance. Headwinds and cold temperatures exaggerate this effect. When riding slowly there is less of an immediate benefit when aerodynamics are improved, but as you are out on the road longer, this improvement can compound to save significant time and energy.

An optimal bike position for triathlon is one that allows you to reach the end of the bike leg in the fastest possible time and feeling the most fresh for the run. Your optimal position will evolve over time. Mike Hanseen, a top bike fit specialist at Canyon Bicycles, in Salt Lake City, recommends that all triathletes get a bike fit once each year. "This is especially important for newbie triathletes experiencing rapid improvements in their skills. They will benefit from a new fit after only a few

ROAD BIKES VERSUS TRI BIKES

The difference between road bikes and tri bikes can be hazy. In fact, perennial Ironman® Canada winner Lori Bowden often raced triathlons on a Specialized Allez frame, which has stock road bike geometry. A tri bike is one designed to be ridden in an aerodynamic position, and a road bike is designed to be ridden in a more upright position. Tri bikes generally have a seat-tube angle of 78 to 81 degrees, shifting a rider forward into an aerodynamic position while maintaining 90-degree angles at the hips and shoulders. Road bikes typically have a seat-tube angle of about 74 degrees, putting the rider in a more upright position while maintaining 90-degree hip and shoulder angles. Road bikes are easier to control in technical situations, such as corners, and put the rider in a more powerful climbing position. Tri bikes enhance aerodynamics at the cost of power production and comfort. This leads to a faster bike split in most races. Both types of bikes have their specialties, and you need to decide which one is right for you. If you have no budget constraints, one of each design is the perfect choice. Tri bikes are faster, road bikes are more nimble. What do you need most?

months," says Hanseen. If you change focus from short-course to long-course triathlons, you should relax your position by raising your aerobars slightly. If you take up yoga and increase your flexibility, you may be able to drop your aerobars into a more aerodynamic position without sacrificing comfort, efficiency, or power.

PHOTO 2.1 *Professional triathlete Lori Bowden racing on a standard road frame*

STANDARD TRIATHLON BIKE POSITION SETUP

There is no standard triathlon setup, but the following information provides a good starting point.

- Start with a 78-degree seat-tube angle.
- Set the cleat position on your shoe so the pedal axle aligns with the ball of your foot.
- Try to achieve a knee angle of 145 to 155 degrees when the crank is near the bottom of the pedal stroke and in line with the seat tube.
- Your knee should be over the pedal axle at 3 o'clock.
- A 90-degree shoulder angle should be formed by your upper arm and torso.
- A 90-degree hip angle should be formed by your torso and leg.
- The drop between the seat and elbow pads should be adjusted for your comfort.

CUSTOMIZE YOUR SETUP

The standard setup will likely provide you with a close fit, but is unlikely the *optimal* setup for you. You will need to customize your setup to meet your unique needs. To determine your optimal position, you must consider your goals, abilities, flexibility, body composition, core strength, and preferences.

Goals. Short-course athletes should give preference to aerodynamics and power production over comfort. Long-course athletes should make comfort their top priority. Top-place finishers should be willing to forgo some comfort in exchange for better aerodynamics and power. Middle- and back-of-the-pack athletes will find more enjoyment by giving comfort a higher priority.

Abilities. Athletes who can generate huge amounts of power may capitalize on that strength and accept a less-aerodynamic position if a more-aero position significantly reduces their power output. Athletes who are less powerful need to take advantage of aerodynamics by making sure it costs them the least possible watts to pedal down the road.

Flexibility. Athletes with superior flexibility will be comfortable and powerful in a more aerodynamic position than athletes who lack flexibility. Less-flexible athletes should position their elbow pads higher in relation to their seat height, so they can breathe easily and avoid discomfort and fatigue in their lower backs.

Body composition. Athletes who have a large upper body mass from either fat or muscle will need to set their elbow pads farther apart and higher in relation to their seat to provide space for their upper body, and will thus be in a less-aerodynamic position than athletes with a slight build.

Core strength. An athlete with superior core strength will retain more power output in an aerodynamic position than one with a weak core. An aerodynamic position is lower and more stretched out, requiring increased core strength to maintain stability and power.

Preferences. Are you a competitor or participator? If you are a competitor seeking optimal performance, you should push the limits with your body position and strive to improve it. If you are a participator, choose comfort over performance.

Achieving Comfort

If your neck hurts, your butt hurts, and your back is stiff, you are not comfortable and you will not ride your fastest. A tri bike will never

TIPS TO INCREASE COMFORT

- Visit a qualified bike fit professional to get your position perfected.
- Select a frame made from a material with top shock-absorbing quality such as titanium.
- Select a beam bike with a shock-absorbing design such as Softride®, brand bikes.
- Increase your flexibility.
- Wear high-quality bike shorts.
- Experiment with different saddles until you find one that is comfortable.
- Increase your core strength.
- Increase your endurance on the bike.

feel like a La-Z-Boy, but you should not be in pain or discomfort. If you are not comfortable, you will waste a lot of energy squirming around on your bike searching for a better position or just trying to ease the pain. If you can't sit in the saddle, you can't possibly put decent power into the pedals, leaving you slow and unhappy.

Achieving Aerodynamics

Since prototype, clip-on aerobars helped Greg LeMond to achieve his famous time-trial victory during the 1989 Tour De France, there has been an increased interest in bicycle aerodynamics. There is a dizzying array of aerodynamic equipment on the market and an equally confusing mass of information available on the subject. Unfortunately, the only way to calculate the aerodynamic drag of your bike and body is to be tested in a wind tunnel. As the vast majority of us do not have ready access to a wind tunnel, we have to use the next best approach—common sense. If it looks clean and smooth then it is probably aero. Use a camera or mirror to look at your position directly from the front. Is there anything obvious sticking out and catching the wind? Do your thighs hide behind your arms? Does one knee splay to the outside, catching the wind? This leg may benefit from a wedge under the shoe to cant it in. Even a baggy jersey or a flapping number will cause drag.

TIPS TO INCREASE AERODYNAMICS

- Ride on your aerobars as much as possible.

- Buy an aerodynamic frame, fork, and wheels.

- Wear tight-fitting clothes.

- Remove any unnecessary parts from your bike, such as water bottle cages.

- Hide your cables.

- Drink from a hydration backpack, not bottles.

- Wear an aerodynamic helmet.

Achieving Power Output

Your position on the bike affects the amount of power you can produce. A position that is too stretched out will rob you of the ability to pedal economically and apply power to the pedals. A common mistake made by beginner triathletes is to slap a set of full-extension aerobars onto a road bike without any additional position adjustments. This will lengthen the cockpit too much, causing back pain, neck pain, and power loss. Intuitively sensing that riding in their "aero" position is inefficient, these triathletes spend the majority of their race riding in their regular road position on the hoods, ignoring their aerobars. Under these circumstances, the aerobars just add up to a chunk of metal that is dragged around the course.

If you do not spend the majority of your ride-time on your aerobars, there is something wrong with your position. To determine the position in which you can generate the most power, you must do some on-bike testing with a power meter (such as a Power-Tap) or put your bike on an indoor trainer (such as a CompuTrainer) that measures power output. Track power output along with position changes to find your optimal position.

A NOTE TO THE ROADIES

A bike position for triathlon is farther forward than a traditional road bike position. If you have been pedaling in a traditional road position for many years, a tri position will feel awkward at first and your performance may suffer temporarily. With some training, you will adjust to the new position and regain your economy. You have to decide if you are willing to make this change. Is triathlon racing your number-one priority? If your answer is yes, you need to change your position. Early in the season, when your training volume is low, is the best time to make the change.

DO-IT-YOURSELF BIKE FIT

To set up your own triathlon racing position, follow these steps in this order:

- Set the position of the cleats on your shoes.
- Determine the appropriate crank length.
- Set your seat height, fore/aft, and tilt position.
- Set your reach.
- Set the seat-to-bar differential.

Cleat Adjustment

There are four important adjustments you can make to your cleat position: the distance along the length of the foot, the position along the width of the foot, the rotation of the cleat, and the cant.

Cleat distance along the length of the foot sets the fore/aft foot position on the pedal. The starting point is to have the cleat attached to the shoe so that the ball of your foot is aligned with the pedal spindle. Moving the cleat toward the heel of the shoe has the effect of moving the foot forward on the pedal. This position favors cyclists who prefer to ride at a high cadence. Moving the cleat toward the toe of the shoe has the effect of moving the foot back on the pedal. In this position, increased ankling can be used to access the calf muscles and put more power into each pedal stroke. Riders who pedal at lower cadences will prefer this position. Cleats moved forward make the foot into a longer lever. It becomes increasingly difficult to stabilize the foot on the pedal resulting in strain on the Achilles tendon and calf muscles.

Cleat distance along the width of the foot sets how close or far from the crank arm your foot sits when clipped into the pedal. Set the cleat so your foot and ankle come close to but do not touch the crank arm during pedaling.

Cleat rotation sets the horizontal-plane angle your foot makes when clipped into the pedal. This angle is important for your knee health. The rotation you set should reflect the angle your feet assume while sitting on the bike in a riding position. If your feet splay out, rotate the front of the cleat toward the medial side of the shoe. If you are pigeon-toed, rotate the front of the cleat toward the lateral side of the shoe. Most cleat systems have a certain degree of float, allowing the foot to find its natural angle while pedaling.

Cant is the vertical-plane angle your foot makes when clipped into the pedal. Excessive canting (like a canoe rocking side to side) is inefficient and may cause injury. The knee will follow the ankle with a lateral motion, rocking in and out with each pedal cycle. A splayed-out knee will catch the wind and reduce aerodynamics. Placing a canted wedge between your cleat and shoe or inserting orthotics inside the shoe will provide stability and reduce wasteful movement. Another option is Look's CX-7 pedal. It is adjustable for pronation and supination, giving the benefit of wedges without increasing stack height.

If your knees splay out while pedaling, canting your foot in will increase your biomechanical efficiency.

Crank Length

Crank length is the distance from the pedal axle to the bottom-bracket axle and determines the diameter of the circle the pedals create when they are moving. Longer cranks allow more power to be applied, and shorter cranks allow higher-cadence pedaling. The larger the pedal circle, the more flexion is required of your knee to get over the top of the pedal stroke. Cranks that are too long may hurt your knees by causing excessive flex, or they may cause your knees to hit your chest in the aero position. Taller people need longer cranks, but larger bikes usually do not come with proportionally longer cranks. The cycling industry gravitates toward medium, so taller and shorter riders may need to ask for different cranks than those that come with the bike. (Many shops will switch cranks at no additional charge.) Most commercially made cranks are only available in lengths of 165 to 180 mm.

Measure your inseam to find your optimum crank length. Stand barefoot with your back to a wall, hold a book up in your crotch, and have an assistant measure the distance from the top of the book to the floor in centimeters. Multiply the inseam measurement by 1.25 and add 65 to calculate your optimal crank length in millimeters.

Crank length (mm) = (1.25 x inseam measurement in cm) + 65

Seat Position

Seat adjustment affects muscle-recruitment patterns, biomechanical efficiency, risk of injury, and comfort. To set your correct seat position, put your bike on a stationary trainer and level it with a carpenter's level.

Seat height is measured from the top center of the seat to the center of the bottom-bracket axle. Ride until you are warmed up and comfortably settled into the saddle. Stop pedaling with one pedal near the bottom of the pedal cycle and with the crank arm in line with the seat tube. Hold your ankle at the angle you pedal. Have an assistant measure the angle formed at your knee by your upper and lower leg using a goniometer. Set your seat height so this angle is 145 to 155 degrees.

Fore/aft seat position, or saddle setback, is a horizontal line measured from the nose of the seat to the center of the bottom bracket.

Measure this distance by dropping a plumb line from the nose of the seat and recording the distance from the plumb line to the center of the bottom bracket. Correct saddle setback is key to placing you in the most efficient position for pedaling. In a strong climbing position, your knee will be directly over the pedal axle during the most powerful point of the pedal cycle—the 3 o'clock position. However, this knee-over-the-spindle position is a "road" position. Most triathletes should be in a more aggressive (farther forward) position, which often allows for a lower handlebar and may reduce hamstring contribution on the bike and enable faster run splits.

To adjust saddle setback, ride until you are warmed up and comfortably settled into the saddle. Stop pedaling with the crank arms horizontal. (Use a carpenter's level to check that the crank arms are horizontal.) Hold your ankle at the angle you pedal. Have an assistant drop a plumb line from the groove made by the patella and the vastus medialis muscle on the front of the knee. This plumb line should intersect or fall in front of the pedal axle, so move the seat forward and back on the seat post until it does. Each time you move the seat forward or back you must reset the seat height. As you move the seat forward it brings you closer to the bottom bracket, and the seat must be raised to preserve the knee angle. Conversely, moving the seat back requires it to be lowered.

Seat tilt is measured in degree deviations from horizontal. Use a level to set the seat in a completely horizontal position and then adjust it from there. Most riders are most comfortable when the nose of the saddle tilts slightly downward. If you tilt the nose down too much, however, you will constantly slide forward, which wastes energy, reduces your economy, and can cause chafing.

Reach

Reach is the distance from the rear of the seat to the center of the handlebars or to the tip of the aerobars. Adjust your reach to achieve a 90-degree hip angle and a 90-degree shoulder angle. The hip angle is formed by your upper leg at the bottom of the pedal stroke with the crank arm in line with the seat tube and your torso. The shoulder angle is formed by your torso and upper arm. Elbow angle is made by the upper and lower arm. A good elbow angle is about 110 degrees. Reach is adjusted by changing stem length, adjusting aerobar length, or switching to a frame with a longer or shorter top tube. Do not adjust your reach by sliding the saddle forward, as this will throw off your position over the pedals.

Seat-to-Bar Differential

Seat-to-bar differential is a vertical line measured from the top center of the seat to the center of the handlebars or elbow pads on the aerobars. To take this measurement, place a level on the seat and

SADDLE SORES

"Saddle sore" is an umbrella term that covers any pain in your crotch that lasts longer than your ride. Boils, hot spots, abrasion, chafing, bruises, rashes, abscesses, carbuncles, and ulcerated skin are all considered saddle sores. These problems will affect your ability to sit comfortably on the saddle and will seriously compromise your cycling ability. Squirming around in your saddle trying to get comfortable takes a lot of energy away from the pedals. The worst-case scenario is that pain will keep you off your bike altogether. The best tactic is prevention. Follow these tips to steer clear of saddle sores:

- Wear clean bike shorts on every ride. Sweaty shorts harbor bacteria and other crotch critters that can cause infection.

- Wear high-quality bike shorts.

- Wear gender-specific shorts. Women should look for shorts that do not have a center seam in the chamois.

- Rotate the brand of shorts you wear daily to avoid friction areas typical with one brand.

- Apply a lubricant, such as Udder Butter or Bag Balm (available at most grocery stores and pharmacies), to high-friction areas before sores develop.

- Do not wear underwear beneath your bike shorts.

- Change out of your sweaty bike shorts immediately after riding.

- Shower right after your ride, using antibacterial soap. If you can't shower right away, wash with antibacterial wipes.

- Wear loose-fitting clothes after your ride to let your skin breathe.

extend it over the handlebars in a horizontal position. Measure the distance from the level down to the center of the handlebars or elbow pads. Adjustments can be made by lowering or raising the stem. Generally, the greater the differential (lower bars), the more aerodynamic and less comfortable the position is. To find the ideal seat-to-bar differential, set the bars at a comfortable height and gradually lower from there.

Treating saddle sores

Saddle sores come in two varieties, open sores and painful areas deep in the tissue, and each requires different treatment.

Open sores, with raw or broken skin, are caused by chafing, which is usually due to friction with your shorts. Eliminate these hot spots by changing to a different brand of shorts and by applying lubricant on the area to reduce friction while riding. For open saddle sores, nothing beats maximum-strength antibiotic ointment such as Neosporin (note: do not get the cream, get the ointment). It provides lubrication, pain relief, and also protects you from infection. After riding, clean saddle sores thoroughly with antibacterial soap and pile on a fresh layer of antibiotic ointment. As a desperate, race-day measure, you can pad the sore with a non-stick, moist, burn pad such as Spenco® 2nd Skin and apply a topical xylocaine to numb the sore for a few hours. Keep a small tube of the topical in your jersey pocket and apply it as needed until the race is over.

Painful areas and lumps deep in the tissue can be very belligerent and hang around for an entire season—if not years. The skin and subcutaneous fat between your bones and the saddle get compressed while riding and blood is reduced (ischemia). Compressed tissue is highly susceptible to infection, heals poorly, and can break down and form a sore just from ischemia, without any infection at all. These sores are similar to "bed sores" and are usually caused by a poorly fit or worn-out saddle that applies extreme pressure to a localized area. Saddles deteriorate over time, so replace yours periodically. A seat set too high will make you rock side to side to reach the pedals, which can also cause you pain. Ignoring a saddle sore can lead to a visit with your doctor to have it lanced and drained, accompanied by a course of antibiotics and a prescription to stay off your bike.

BIKE SETUP TIP

When you are setting up a new bike, stack a few spacers between the head tube and stem. This enables you to lower the handlebars and improve aerodynamics at a later date—a good option for athletes who race all distances of triathlon in one season. Simply move the spacers to the top of the stem to lower the handlebars for a more aerodynamic position, or stack them below the stem to boost handlebar height for more comfort.

Aerobar Setup

You should have already determined the length of your aerobars when adjusting your reach. The optimal tilt of your aerobars and the position of the elbow pads depend upon torso angle. Flexible triathletes who can ride in an aggressive position will have a torso angle close to horizontal. Less-flexible athletes will be more comfortable and powerful in a more upright position and have a torso angle up to 45 degrees from horizontal. Torso angle dictates how much of the chest area is exposed to the wind.

Aggressive position aerobar setup

Athletes who can achieve a horizontal torso should have horizontal aerobars. Wind-tunnel testing has shown horizontal aerobars to be superior to bars that tilt up. An upward-tilted aerobar deflects turbulent air down onto the legs, causing additional drag. Some triathletes prefer a slight downward tilt of the aerobars, as it can provide a good position for leverage. The elbow pads should hit your forearm comfortably just in front of the elbow. If the pads are too far up your forearm, they will not provide a good base of support. The distance the pads are set apart from each other is important from an aerodynamic standpoint. When viewed from the front, your elbows should sit inside the shadow of your thighs. Moving the elbows into a position narrower than this does not have significant aero benefits and can decrease comfort, the ability to breathe easily, and power production. The most aero position for an athlete who can get horizontal (shoulders as low as hips) is with arms thigh-width apart so that the legs can maximally draft the arms.

Relaxed position aerobar setup

Athletes with a torso angle closer to 45 degrees have an increased area of chest exposed to the wind. Redirecting the wind around this chest cavity is the top aerodynamic priority. An aerobar tilted slightly up will close this chest cavity, as will bringing the elbows closer together. It is critical for less-flexible athletes to set the elbow pads so the outside of the upper arm is at least as narrow as the outside of the torso. Narrowing to this point will produce huge benefits. Going narrower will still provide incremental benefits but not to the same degree. When you narrow your elbow position, do so gradually by no more than a half-centimeter every two months.

CUSTOM BIKE FIT

An even better way to achieve the best fit and position on your bike is to schedule an appointment with a bike fit specialist. (See the sidebar on page 30 for tips on finding the best technician for you.) Before getting started, the specialist should understand your intended use for the bike and your race goals as well as your body type, flexibility, riding style, and preferences.

If you are an experienced cyclist with many years of pedaling in your legs, you may be stuck in a position groove. When a specialist moves you into a new position, it may feel awkward at first and your race times may slow initially. Trust the specialist and stick with the position for a few weeks, giving your body time to adjust. What is familiar to us is not always what is best for us.

There are two ways a bike fit specialist can work with you to set up your optimal bike position. Option number one is obviously the best choice.

Before you purchase a bike, visit a specialist for a professional bike fit and positioning session. Top bike shops usually own a Serrota fit cycle. This is a stationary bike with moveable frame tubes, parts, and angles, enabling the technician to determine a perfect fit and position for you. Once your fit has been found and your measurements have been recorded, the specialist will help you find a bike to purchase and set it up exactly according to your measurements.

A specialist can also adapt your current bike to meet your needs, moving you into an optimal position to help you achieve your race goals.

HOW TO LOCATE THE BEST BIKE FIT SPECIALIST

Choose a bike fit specialist and positioning technician carefully. To start your search, contact local USA Triathlon– and USA Cycling–certified coaches and ask for their recommendations. Links to these coaches can be found at www.usatriathlon.org and www.bicyclecoach.com. Also, ask around on training rides and at races for advice, as other iders are often the best source of information.

Once you have located a technician with a good reputation, ask about his or her bike fit experience and certifications. There are several bike fit certifications available; two of the best are F.I.S.T. (Fit Institute Slowtwitch) and Serrota Fit Expert.

Dan Empfield, founder of Quintana Roo and the inventor of triathlon-specific bikes, suggests asking a fit technician many questions. "If you were diagnosed with brain cancer and you needed a surgeon, you'd ask questions. You'd see BEFORE the surgery whether this surgeon seemed to know his stuff, had a proper attitude, etc. Okay, bike fit's not brain surgery. But to the degree that this is important to you, I'd ask questions."

A professional bike fit will cost in the range of $50 to $400 and is a worthwhile investment. You may not feel like laying out $100 today for a bike fit, but if you are uncomfortable at mile 50 of an ironman, I guarantee you would pay 10 times that amount for some relief. Most bike shops will rebate the cost of the bike fit when you buy a new bike from them, or they will give you a money-back guarantee if the bike fit does not work for you.

PHOTO **2.2** *Serrota fit cycle*

Becoming educated about bike position is important so you know how to optimize your bike position in response to changes in your goals or your body. Also, the more knowledge you have, the better you can assist your bike fit specialist in achieving the best position for you.

RETROFITTING YOUR ROAD BIKE FOR TRIATHLON RACING

Many athletes enter triathlon racing on a standard road bike. After completing the distance, they naturally look for improved performances at subsequent races. One key area to improve is equipment selection. If it is not in your budget to buy a new bike, there are many things you can do to your road bike to retrofit it for triathlons. In fact, some top triathletes prefer road-geometry frames and have them set up for triathlon racing.

The basic difference between road and tri bikes is that tri bikes have a geometry that sets the rider in an aerodynamic position while preserving hip and shoulder angle. A triathlon bike has a steep seat-tube angle, which rotates the rider forward into a lower and more aerodynamic position than a road bike.

Attach Aerobars

Simply bolting a pair of aerobars onto your road bike is the first step to achieving increased aerodynamics. As was mentioned before, the problem with this is it leaves you too stretched out as you reach for your aerobars, resulting in a loss of power and comfort. The power loss is primarily caused by reducing the hip angle to less than 90 degrees, making it hard to pedal with good form over the top of the pedal stroke. In addition, the torso may be crunched up at the hips, making it difficult to breathe, and the knees may even hit the stomach.

Shorten Your Cockpit

To fully optimize your road bike for triathlon racing and riding on the aerobars, you must shorten your cockpit to achieve 90-degree angles at your hip and shoulder. You can shorten your reach by sliding the seat forward, raising the handlebars, choosing short-length aerobars, or switching to a shorter stem. However, more weight will be distributed onto the front wheel when you move your seat forward, which may make your bike unstable. A forward seat position may feel odd to an experienced road cyclist—like you are pedaling with your feet behind your hips. This can be adapted to, but there comes a point along the sliding-the-seat-forward continuum where efficiency is sacrificed. Short-length aerobars, such as the Profile Design Jammer GT, work well to shorten the cockpit.

Dedicate a Front End

A dedicated front end will allow easy changes between road and tri positions. A front end consists of your stem and handlebars. One front end can have a road stem and bar and the other setup can have a tri-position stem and aerobars. To make switching the front ends a cinch, add couplers to your cables. All you need to do to change from road to tri setup is insert the stem, couple the cables, slide your seat forward, and raise it appropriately.

MOUNTAIN BIKE FIT

Due to the technically challenging terrain and lower average speeds of mountain biking, priority should be given to bike agility and handling ease over aerodynamics. Comfort and power output are also important factors. A mountain bike race position is somewhat more aggressive (lower in the front) than a recreational mountain bike position. A lower front end effectively moves a rider's center of gravity forward and more evenly distributes weight over the front and rear wheels. In this position, riders can respond to uphills and downhills by moving their weight forward and backward respectively. Balance and weight shifts keep the tires in contact with the ground and enable a rider to power the pedals with good tire-to-ground traction.

A mountain bike race position is similar to a standard road cycling position.

PART TWO

Training Your Body

C H A P T E R

3 Flexibility and Core Strength

Greater flexibility will allow you to achieve a lower, more aerodynamic position without sacrificing comfort or power production. Greater core strength creates a stable platform from which you can transfer your leg power into the pedals. When combined, increased core strength and flexibility allow you to remain quiet, stable, and comfortable for a long time, while powering the pedals in a low, aerodynamic position. Core strength and flexibility are intertwined with one another. Developing them both together in a combined program will teach your body how to be strong and flexible at the same time. This will increase your agility—a basic skill needed for fluid and economical movement in any sport.

During races, a weak core will show up as a dull ache in the lower back that never goes away. Once compromised, the core muscles cannot stabilize the torso. When your torso is no longer stable, it cannot provide your legs with a solid platform from which to power the pedals, and your power output will begin to decrease. A sore lower back may cause you to stop pedaling to stretch and squirm into a new position in an attempt to access muscles that are not yet fatigued. The net result is a slower bike split and a slow transition to running.

FLEXIBILITY

There are several types of stretching: static, ballistic, and PNF (proprioceptive neuromuscular function), all of which have been scientifically proven to increase flexibility. There is no agreement on which method is superior, but it is generally agreed that static stretching is the safest. Ballistic stretching must be performed with extreme caution, because it can cause muscle- or tendon-strain injuries. Recent research is debunking the long-held belief that stretching before and after exercise reduces muscle soreness and the risk of injury. Stretching to prevent muscle injury and muscle soreness is not supported by evidence from clinical research studies. Several studies have actually shown muscle strength to be reduced after stretching. A 2001 study reported in the *Canadian Journal of Applied Physiology* demonstrated muscle strength losses of 12 percent, 10 minutes after stretching. Repeated maximal stretching can decrease strength for up to an hour. This means that maximal stretching before training or racing is not a good idea.

Why Stretch?

If stretching reduces muscle strength and does not prevent muscle soreness and injury, why should you stretch? The sport of triathlon does not have extreme flexibility demands like a sport such as gymnastics, yet stretching is important for economy, recovery, and aerodynamics.

Economy. Permanent increases in flexibility will decrease passive muscle tension. For a cyclist, that means during the pedal stroke it takes less force to lengthen a flexible hamstring than an inflexible one. Increased flexibility will therefore increase your pedaling economy.

Recovery. Stretching will speed recovery from workouts. Several studies have shown that stretching stimulates the passage of amino acids into muscle cells, accelerates protein synthesis inside the cells, and inhibits protein degradation. Post-workout stretching helps muscle cells repair themselves and synthesize energy-producing enzymes and structures, which enhances overall fitness.

Aerodynamics. The number-one reason for triathletes to stretch is to achieve a more aerodynamic position on the bike without sacrificing power or comfort. Flexibility is a requirement for a good, aggressive, aero position, which will reduce your bike splits and improve your performance.

> ## GORDO BYRN ON THE IMPACT OF FLEXIBILITY
>
> One of my goals last winter was to improve my flexibility. My main reason for wanting to do this was to be able to get myself into a more aerodynamic cycling position. I am happy to report that after just three months I removed an inch of spacers from my race bike and had to jack my seat up half an inch (my legs "dropped" when my hips released). I believe that I will be able to go even lower (comfortably), when I buy my new TT bike in the spring. My 2002 Kiwi race bike was steeper than my Ironman® Canada 2001 race bike, so I expect that my new position will be worth several minutes of free speed—at least as much as a set of race wheels.
>
> Gordo Byrn is a professional triathlete and Ultraman winner and co-author of *Going Long: Training for Ironman-Distance Triathlons.*

When to Stretch

The best time to stretch is immediately after a workout, because it's important to stretch a warm muscle. Stretching before a workout isn't the best idea, as several studies have shown an increased incidence of injury in athletes who stretch prior to workouts. These injuries may occur during stretching or be a consequence of working out with reduced muscle strength following a stretching session. Do not do a session of serious stretching within the hour prior to a race or a hard workout.

How to Stretch

To develop flexibility, static stretches should be held for 20 to 30 seconds and performed daily. "Little and often" is a good maxim for stretching. Stretch a muscle until you feel it lengthen. As you feel the muscle tension ease during a stretch you can gently reach farther, but if you feel any pain you are being too aggressive and should back off. Follow the muscle as it releases, and do not force it to stretch faster than it wants. Some muscles, especially overworked or postural hip muscles, may take longer than 30 seconds to release. Breathing is important; relax and breathe slowly and deeply as you stretch. You should never hold a position beyond where you can comfortably breathe. Don't overdo it! Moderate stretching routines work better than aggressive ones.

A 10-Minute Post-Ride Stretching Routine

Develop the habit of stretching after every ride. After hard and long workouts, sip a recovery drink while you are stretching. The following is a 10-minute stretching routine to do after a ride. This is a good routine from which to build, but you should seek additional stretches to target your personal stretching needs. Do each of the following stretches once after riding.

Quadriceps

The quadriceps are a major cycling muscle group. They are comprised of four muscles located in the front of the thigh. Stretch them as follows: While standing, pull one foot up to your buttocks; keep your knees together, and hold the stretch for 20 seconds. This will stretch the three vastus quadriceps muscles in the front of your thigh.

Next, keep hold of your foot, move the knee of the stretching leg behind you without leaning forward, and hold this position for 20 seconds. This will stretch the rectus femoris muscle, which is the top of the quadriceps.

Calves

Face a wall (placing your hands on it for stability if needed) and take one step back with the leg to be stretched. Push the heel of the leg behind you toward the floor and hold the stretch for 20 seconds.

Psoas

The psoas is a groin muscle. It originates on the lumbar spine (lower back), travels over the front of the pelvis, and inserts on the femur (thigh bone). The main job of the psoas muscle in cycling is to get the leg up the back side and over the top of the pedal stroke. The psoas can become very tight in cyclists, but it is often overlooked in a stretching routine. Tightness and weakness in the psoas muscle are the primary causes of dull ache in the lower back on long rides.

Stretch the psoas as follows: Put your front foot on a low bench, turn your back foot out, and press your hips forward and toward the floor. Hold this position for 20 seconds. You should feel this stretch on the front side of the hip and inner thigh of your rear leg.

Hamstrings and lower back

The hamstrings are located on the rear of your thigh. Stretch them and your lower back as follows: Sit on the floor with your legs straight out in front of you and lean forward until you

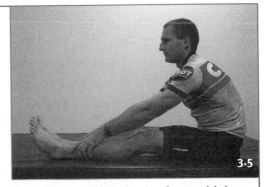

feel a gentle stretch in your lower back and the back of your thighs. Rotate your pelvis forward to increase the stretch in your hamstrings, and hold the stretch for 20 seconds.

Hip and illiotibial band (ITB)

Lie on your back, pull one knee into your chest, and roll it over your torso toward the floor on the opposite side, keeping your shoulders flat on the floor. Hold the stretch for 20 seconds.

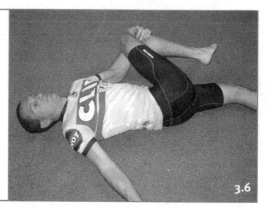

3.6

Adductors

Sit on the floor with the soles of your feet together, and pull your heels close to your buttocks. Lean forward with a flat back and hold for 20 seconds. You should feel this stretch in your inner thighs. To increase the stretch, place your elbows on your knees and gently push them toward the floor.

3.7

Abdomen, shoulders, and back

Kneel on the floor, place your hands on a chair, and drop your shoulders down toward the floor until you feel a stretch in your shoulders and abdomen. Hold the stretch for 20 seconds.

3.8

On-Bike Stretching

During long-distance events, it is helpful to stretch on the bike periodically to keep the working muscles flexible. On-bike stretching should be brief and gentle. Start stretching after you've been riding for 15 minutes, and repeat your stretches every 15 minutes thereafter. Downhill sections of road where you can coast are good places to stretch. To stretch your calves, drop your heels down behind the pedal. Your lower back can be stretched by standing up, and arching your lower back like a cat. While standing, move your pelvis in circles (like Elvis) in both directions. You can relieve neck tension by sitting up and briefly bringing your chin to your chest. (Be sure to look where you are going while you do this.)

CORE TRAINING

Your core is defined as your abdominals, lower back, buttocks, and hips. The abdominal muscle group is made up of four muscles: rectus abdominis, transverse abdominis, internal obliques, and external obliques. Each of these muscles serves a specific function in movement and stability. The ever-popular crunch exercise isolates and strengthens the rectus abdominis only. Core strengthening programs consisting only of crunches result in weakness in the other three abdominal muscles and other key core muscles in the back and hips. All of the core muscles must act together to stabilize the spine. Think beyond crunches.

Stabilize or Mobilize

There are two ways to strengthen the core. The first method is to repeatedly flex, extend, and rotate the trunk as in traditional crunch exercises. The second method is to stabilize the trunk against a force. For example, the plank exercise stabilizes the trunk against the force of gravity. Triathletes often feel if they are not moving then they must not be training. However, to appropriately train your core you have to think outside that box. It is crucial to train the core muscles in the way you plan to use them. When you are cycling, your core musculature stabilizes your trunk against the force of gravity and the force of your legs rotating the cranks. To appropriately train your core for cycling, you need to incorporate both mobilization and stabilization exercises into your routine.

Sample Core Training Routine

The best way to train your core is to build a large repertoire of exercises so that you can do a different routine each time. You are only limited by your imagination. Vary the exercises you select, the speed in which you do them, the length of time you stabilize, and the amount of force you stabilize against. Continually challenge your core in new ways. The main principles to follow when creating a routine are to exercise the entire core during each session, not just the rectus abdominis muscle, and to include stabilization exercises in every session.

A sample core training routine follows.

TIPS FOR CORE STRENGTHENING EXERCISES

- Contract your abdominal muscles throughout all exercises. Think of keeping your belly button pressed into your spine. This presses your muscles close to your spinal column and provides spinal support.

- During exercises when your feet are up off the floor, keep your belly button pressed into your spine and your spine pressed into the floor to support your lumbar spine.

- During exercises when your feet are on the floor, keep your pelvis and your spine in a neutral position.

- Target your whole core by alternating abdominal, back, and side exercises.

- Include stabilization and flexion-extension exercises.

- Include exercises that target the psoas muscle.

- Move fluidly without throwing and jerking motions.

- Breathe slowly and smoothly throughout exercises.

- Add lots of variety to your core training routine.

Oblique crunch

Lie on your back with your left foot flat on the floor and your right ankle over your left knee. Lift your head and shoulders, rotate your torso to the right as you rise up in a controlled movement, and then lower. Keep your neck in a neutral position and don't pull on your head. Alternate sides and vary the tempo. Exhale as you lift and inhale as you lower, controlling your mus-

cles throughout the entire movement. Lift and rotate only as high as your abdominal muscles will take you, and avoid recruiting your arms or other muscles to throw your torso higher.

Psoas crunch

Kneel on all fours with one end of an elastic exercise band (swim cords work great here) tied to your right ankle and the other end tied to an attachment point beyond your feet. Extend your left arm and right leg out and then crunch them in, bringing your left elbow toward your right knee. Round your back, exhale, and pull your belly button up to your spine as you

crunch. Hold this position for two seconds and repeat. To add variety to this exercise, support your arms on an exercise ball instead of the floor, or turn over and do this exercise lying on your back.

Swimming

Lie on your front with your arms stretched out over-head. Pull your abdominal muscles in toward your spine and keep them engaged

3.13

throughout the exercise. Straighten your arms and legs and keep them straight throughout the exercise. Raise your arms and legs two inches off the floor. Beat your arms and legs up and down as if splashing water. Move your right arm and left leg down while your left arm and right leg move up. Breathe smoothly and vary the tempo.

Hip circles

Sit on the floor with your legs extended in front of you. Lean back and sup-port yourself on your arms. Contract your abdominals and round your lower back slightly. Lift your legs off the ground and hold your body in a V-shape. Draw a large circle with your legs and then switch direction. This is an advanced exer-cise. If your lower back arches or you feel pain any-where, do not do this exer-cise until you have built up the strength for it.

3.14

3.15

Front plank

Hold and stabilize in the front plank position (as shown in Photo 3.16) for up to 10 long, smooth breaths. For a more advanced version, lift and lower your right leg in a controlled movement while keeping your hips and torso perfectly still (see Photo 3.17). Repeat with your left leg.

Side plank

Sit on the floor with your legs extended to one side and your elbow on the floor for support on the other side. Raise your torso and straighten your legs into a side plank position (see Photo 3.18). Pause and stabilize in this position, with your abdominals contracted, for up to 10 smooth, long breaths and then lower.

Make sure your hips remain stacked on top of each other. Leaning backward or forward is cheating. To add variety to this exercise, lift one leg as shown in Photo 3.19. Alternate upper and lower legs when doing the one-leg-only version.

Reverse plank

Sit on the floor with your legs extended in front of you. Lean back and support your weight on your arms. Straighten your legs and torso into the reverse plank position as shown in Photo 3.20. Pause and stabilize in this position with your abdominals contracted for up to 10 smooth long breaths and then lower. For a more advanced version, lift and lower your right leg in a controlled movement while keeping your hips and torso perfectly still as shown in Photo 3.21. Repeat with your left leg.

Core Training Exercise Menu
Stability exercises

Front, side, and reverse planks. See previous descriptions and Photos 3.16–3.21.

Breaststroke. Lie on your front with your arms stretched out overhead. Pull your abdominal muscles in toward your spine and keep them locked in throughout the whole exercise. Lift your arms two inches off the ground, then arc them around to your sides in a breaststroke fashion while lifting your chest and chin. Hold here and stabilize, then dive your head down and your arms forward again in a breaststroke fashion back to the start. Breathe as if in water. Inhale as you lift, stroke back and exhale as you dive forward.

Heel beats. Lie on your front with your arms stretched out overhead. Pull your abdominal muscles in toward your spine and keep them locked in throughout the whole exercise. Straighten your arms and legs and keep them straight throughout the whole exercise. Raise your arms and legs two inches off the floor. Clap your heels 20 times, rest, stretch, and repeat.

Front crawl. Lie on your front with your arms stretched out over-head. Pull your abdominal muscles in toward your spine and keep them locked in throughout the whole exercise. Raise your arms and legs two inches off the floor. Hold your left arm and both legs still. Drop only the fingertips of your right hand to the floor and lightly drag them along the floor toward your right shoulder. Raise your elbow up as high as you can toward the ceiling as your arm comes in. Continue dragging your fingertips along the floor and graze your thumb along your side until your arm is extended straight toward your feet. Pause and stabilize here. Feel the opposition stretch as your left arm reaches forward and your right arm stretches back. Reverse the finger drag forward, making sure to keep your elbow high. Repeat with your left arm. Exhale as you stroke back and inhale as you stroke forward. To reduce the intensity, keep your legs on the floor.

Mobility exercises

Crunches. Lie on your back with your knees bent and your feet flat on the floor. Lift your head and shoulders off the floor using your abdominals, and then lower them. Keep your neck in a neutral position and don't pull on your head. Vary the tempo. Increase the intensity by lifting your feet off the floor.

Side crunches. Lie on your side with your legs straight and your arms relaxed. Lift your shoulders and legs at same time, and then lower them. Vary the tempo.

Reverse crunch. Lie on your back, press your lower back to the floor, and hold your legs with a 90-degree bend at the hips and knees. Curl your tailbone off the floor using your lower abs, then lower your legs while maintaining the 90-degree bend at your hips and knees.

Standing trunk-twist. Hold a stick on your shoulders (not on your neck) behind your head. Rotate your torso from side to side like a periscope in a slow, controlled manner. Keep your hips facing forward. There should be no rotation in your legs and knees.

Hanging knee-raise. Hang from a pull-up bar or dip station. Contract your core muscles and lift your knees as high as you can without throwing them. Control the motion while you raise and lower your knees. Vary the tempo.

Seated knee-raise. Sit at the very end of a bench. Lean back a bit and round your lower back slightly. With bent knees, lift both feet two inches off the floor. Pull one knee toward your chest, then extend back to the start. Alternate legs, keep your core contracted, and do not let your back arch.

Dumbbell side-bend. Stand with a dumbbell in one hand. Lower the dumbbell down your thigh as far as you can without leaning forward or backward and then return to an upright position.

Roll-ups. Lie on your back with your legs straight and your arms extended overhead. Exhale as you roll up to a sitting position. Lift your arms first, then your head, followed by your shoulders. Continue to roll up and forward, concentrating on one vertebrae at a time. Inhale as you stretch forward, keeping your belly button pressed to your spine. Exhale and roll back down slowly and with control, exhaling throughout the whole movement. Stretch tall, inhale, and repeat. Think of curling yourself forward, stretching, and then slowly uncurling back down onto the mat. Move with a smooth, fluid motion at a constant speed. Avoid throwing your body up, or allowing it to flop down. Keep your heels on the floor at all times.

Roll-over. Lie on your back with your arms by your sides and your legs held up toward the ceiling. Inhale to prepare and then exhale slowly as you contract your lower abs and peel your spine off the mat one vertebra at a time, starting from your tailbone. Inhale and hold when you have lifted as far as you can, then exhale as you lower yourself back to the starting position with your legs straight up toward the ceiling. Control the movement and move fluidly, avoiding any throwing or jerking motions. Do not roll onto the back of your neck, but balance on your shoulders instead. Make sure you are lifting from the back of your hips and not simply allowing the weight of your legs to pull you over. Only curl your pelvis up as much as your muscle strength will allow.

Back extensions. Back extensions using an exercise ball are a great way to build strength. Lie face down with the ball under your hips and your hands and feet on the floor. Keep your feet on the floor and lift your upper body to a neutral spine position. Avoid hyperextending your spine. For variety, add rotation movements. As you lift, turn your shoulders to the side or try figure eight rotations with your shoulders.

As with all new exercises, start slowly and avoid any movement that causes any pain. If you are not confident in your technique, seek the services of a certified personal trainer.

Psoas Muscle Exercises

Be sure to add core training exercises into your routine that specifically strengthen the psoas muscle, such as psoas crunches and variations described earlier. In addition, the following core exercises target the psoas muscle.

Sit-ups. Sit on the floor with your feet hooked under a support and your knees bent. Lower your torso down to the floor, then rise back up using both your abdominal and leg muscles.

Exercise ball pikes. Start in the front plank position with your knees on the top of an exercise ball. Keep your shoulders over your hands and your legs straight as you lift your hips up toward the ceiling and roll the ball toward your arms. Exhale on the lift and pull your abdominals into your spine. Hold at the top for two seconds, then lower and repeat.

Leg drive. Lie on your back with exercise bands connecting your ankles to a point beyond your feet. Raise your shoulders off the ground, pull your belly button into your spine, and press your lumbar spine firmly into the floor Hold this position as you alternate driving your left and then right knee to your chest. To add variety to this exercise, place your hands behind your ears, rotate your torso to the right as your left knee drives up, and then rotate your torso to the left as your right knee drives up. This is an advanced exercise and should only be done if you have the strength to keep your belly button pulled into your spine (to contract your transverse abdominis muscle) and your lower back pressed onto the floor.

Pilates

Developed by Joseph H. Pilates this method focuses on core strength and full body flexibility. It is the perfect method for cyclists to increase their flexibility and strengthen their core in one session. The only equipment you need is a body-size padded mat. Once learned, the Pilates routines can be done anywhere. More in-depth Pilates programs involve more equipment, but for a daily routine the mat work is sufficient. Pilates is based on nine ruling principles: concentration, control, center, fluidity, precision, breath, imagination, intuition, and integration. Each of these principles is also important for peak triathlon performance. To learn the Pilates method, sign up for a class with a certified Pilates trainer. *The Pilates Body* by Brooke Siller is a valuable reference with clear photos and exercise descriptions.

4 Technique, Skills, and Tactics

F R E E   S P E E D : *Improve your technique and you will go faster without any increase in your fitness or level of effort.*

Triathletes have long known that technique is the most important element in swimming speed. Water provides a denser medium than air, amplifying the need for excellent technique. I am sure we have all been beaten out of the water by swimmers we consider to be less fit than ourselves. What they had that we did not was better economy of movement. They were able to move at the same or a faster speed using less energy than we were. In the exercise physiology lab, economy is a rating of submaximal work output in relation to oxygen consumed. For example, if we tested two riders with the same aerobic capacity and discovered that rider A used less oxygen at 300 watts than rider B, we'd say that rider A was more economical.

Joe Friel believes that it's possible for most riders to improve their economy by at least 5 percent, even for experienced riders, and perhaps as much as 20 percent for beginners. Every percentage point of improvement translates into a percentage point of improvement in race fitness. How many intervals would you have to do or miles would you have to log to boost your aerobic capacity or lactate threshold by 5 to 20 percent? That would be a lot of sweat and suffering.

To be fast, an athlete needs perfect technique. If athlete A has better technique than athlete B, he or she will have better economy and go farther and faster on the same amount of fuel. This is just as true for cycling as it is for swimming. Cycling technique can be broken down into three categories: pedaling technique, bike-handling skills, and race tactics.

PEDALING TECHNIQUE

Pedaling economy is all about conserving fuel. An economical rider uses less energy compared with a sloppy pedaler. Economical pedaling comes from the split-second timing of muscle contractions and relaxations. Throughout the pedal stroke, scores of muscles must fire, some longer than others, and then relax. These muscle recruitment patterns are initiated by signals from the central nervous system and are automatic, but they can be improved. Improvement demands frequent repetition. Economy work trains the nervous system. Teaching the nerves to contract and relax muscles at just the right times doesn't happen quickly, but if you are consistent and patient, you will start riding faster. During a one-hour ride, you will revolve your pedals about 5,000 times. Even a very tiny increase in your pedaling economy will have great effects on your speed when multiplied by 5,000.

The Pedal Circle

During each pedal stroke, you have 360 degrees of opportunity to apply force to the pedals. Research from the U.S. Olympic Training Center demonstrates that the average cyclist only effectively uses 60 degrees—from about 3 o'clock to 5 o'clock. The upstroke of the pedal circle is from 6 o'clock to 11 o'clock. An average cyclist's leg weighs about 20 pounds. Leaving that weight resting on the pedal on the upstroke makes the opposite leg have to work to lift it up to the top. This is energy that could be used to propel the bike forward instead.

Biomechanically, we are relatively weak in the upstroke motion. The most efficient method of pedaling through this part of the pedal stroke is simply to "unweight" the pedal. Be light on the upstroke—actively pulling up is a waste of energy.

The two areas of the pedal stroke where most cyclists can make tremendous efficiency gains are at the top and bottom. The top of the pedal stroke, from roughly 11 o'clock to 1 o'clock, is a neglected area. Efficiency research done on cyclists has shown that pushing the pedal forward, then forward and down, produces an effective force; the forward momentum generated is worth the energy cost. On the backstroke, from 5 o'clock to 7 o'clock, you need to pull back. If you are still pushing down when the pedal is at 6 o'clock, you are wasting energy "stretching" the crank.

Mashers and Spinners

The main difference in pedaling style between a "masher" and a "spinner" is the portion of the pedal revolution that is being used effectively. A masher stomps on the pedals from about 2 o'clock through 5 o'clock. A spinner uses more of the pedal stroke by pedaling efficiently, in the way described in the previous paragraph.

Comparing the power outputs of the two styles is interesting. For example, consider two cyclists pedaling 90 pedal revolutions per minute (rpm) and producing an average of 250 watts. One cyclist is a masher and the other a spinner. The peak power output during one pedal revolution for the masher is at 3 o'clock and is 500 watts. The spinner uses more of the pedal stroke and only needs a peak power output of 400 watts during each revolution to maintain an average output of 250 watts. In other words, the masher is revving his engine higher than the spinner to achieve the same average power output. This may be an effective strategy for a very short race, such as a 100m track sprint. For any endurance-based event, however, spinning is the more efficient style.

In addition to pedaling economy, triathletes must consider the effects their pedaling style will have on their running legs. A spinning style puts more stress on the cardiovascular system, while mashing fatigues the muscles. The cardiovascular system has unlimited endurance and will keep on going for a lifetime. Your leg muscles, however, do not have that kind of endurance and will give up on you when you have pushed them too hard or too far. Sparing muscle fatigue by spinning, not mashing, should be a priority during the bike so you start the run with fresh legs.

PREVENTING HAMSTRING FATIGUE DURING CYCLING

by Ken Mierke

Most of a cyclist's power should come from the gluteus maximus and quadriceps muscles during the downstroke. These muscles combine to extend the upper leg at the hip and the lower leg at the knee. Other accessory muscles should be involved, but should not fatigue greatly and certainly should never be a limiting factor in cycling performance.

Many cyclists find the hamstring muscles fatigue quickly when they ride hard. Multisport athletes, in particular, need to be sure to keep their hamstring muscles fresh because they are so crucial for efficient running after the bike. If you suffer from hamstring fatigue while riding, or when you run off the bike, make the following adjustments to your technique. You will be able to ride faster, farther, and without hamstring pain.

The way the hamstring muscles attach creates one difficulty for cyclists. Since the hamstring crosses both the hip and the knee joints, it has two major functions: hip extension and knee flexion. During all 360 degrees of the pedal stroke, a cyclist undergoes either hip extension or knee flexion . . . so the hamstring muscles potentially contract throughout the entire pedal stroke without a moment to recover. No wonder they fatigue for so many riders.

Each muscle involved in the pedal stroke must have periods of relaxation during which they recover from the powerful contractions they have just been required to produce. The key is learning when the hamstrings are required to produce power in an efficient stroke and when they should be relaxed—and then learning to pedal that way.

Downstroke

Most of a cyclist's power is released during the downstroke. This phase of the pedal stroke, when performed properly, overlaps power output from hip extension (gluteus maximus and hamstrings) and knee extension (quadriceps). Misunderstanding how power should be applied during the downstroke causes many riders to lose this crucial overlap and overuse the hamstrings.

Many cyclists begin the downstroke late, at about 2 o'clock and apply the power produced directly downward. This separates the optimal torque ranges of hip extension and knee extension and calls the hamstrings into play excessively. Since the quadricep muscles are not activated properly, almost all the power must be produced by hip extension. To accomplish this, the hamstrings must contract forcefully.

In an ideal downstroke, the power application begins early, at 12 o'clock, and is directed downward diagonally toward 4 o'clock. This activates the quadriceps optimally and lengthens the overlap between the peak-torque production of knee extension and hip extension. The quadriceps and gluteus maximus are the primary power producers and the hamstrings contract moderately.

Backstroke

Power production during this phase of the pedal stroke is critical for effective climbing. Each pedal stroke reaches a crisis moment when one pedal is at 12 o'clock and the other is at 6 o'clock. Since neither leg is engaged in a downstroke, creating a little bit of power in this "dead spot" carries momentum through to the next downstroke.

The backstroke is one area of the pedal stroke where the hamstring muscles should be very active, because only knee flexion provides power in this range. Relaxation during another range of the pedal stroke (upstroke) prevents fatigue and enables powerful backstroke contractions without overusing the hamstrings.

A primary weakness of many riders is extending the downstroke too long and starting the backstroke late. This prevents the rider from unloading before bottom-dead-center and causes wasted energy pushing downward when the crankarm is moving directly backward.

You should begin the backstroke at 3 o'clock, trying to pull the heel straight back, directly through the bottom bracket. Obviously you

continued on next page

PREVENTING HAMSTRING FATIGUE
DURING CYCLING (continued from previous page)

can't do this, but the downstroke is such a naturally dominant aspect of the pedal stroke that it will finish itself without your concentration.

Mentally triggering the backstroke early helps you to unload by bottom-dead-center. Every rider continues to press down at 6 o'clock. Obviously this is wasted energy. Only power directed at a tangent to the arc described by the pedals propels the bike. More economical riders press down at 6 o'clock, having learned to begin the back-stroke earlier. Their power production more closely resembles the back and down arc followed by the pedal. Attempting to begin the backstroke at 3 o'clock gives you the best chance of timing the transition from downstroke to backstroke optimally.

Upstroke

Most cyclists create negative power during the upstroke, actually pushing down on the pedal and negating some of the power of the other leg's downstroke. During steady state riding, efficient riders lift the weight of their foot, leg, and shoe during the upstroke. They avoid creating negative power during this phase. We call this "unloading," and it allows all of the leg's downstroke power to contribute to propulsion instead of wasting energy lifting the opposite leg. This aspect of pedaling is critical. Unloading on the upstroke is one significant difference between elite and intermediate riders. Without correct unloading, the right and left legs actually fight against each other.

The movements of the upstroke are hip flexion (lifting the knee) and knee flexion (lifting the foot). Since the hip flexors are active only in this range of the pedal stroke, they should be the primary muscle contracting during this phase. Since the hamstrings are active during the backstroke and somewhat active during the downstroke, efficient riders relax them during the upstroke phase.

Attempting to pull up on the pedal through this phase places too much concentration on knee flexion and prevents hamstring relaxation. The hip flexors, once trained, are extremely fatigue resistant.

They are only active for about 25 percent of the pedal stroke. Obviously they can contract very powerfully with a 1 to 3 work to rest ratio. Using the hip flexors and not the hamstrings during the upstroke is crucial.

There are two keys to taking advantage of fresh hip-flexor muscles and resting tired hamstring muscles. The first is keeping your concentration on lifting your knee and not your heel or foot. If you think of lifting your heel (or pedal or foot), you are likely to use knee flexion to accomplish the movement. Think of lifting your knee powerfully, and your foot and pedal will follow without contractions to bend the knee.

The second key is thinking of the upstroke as a diagonally upward and forward movement, instead of an upward and backward movement. Again, this places the emphasis on your hip-flexor muscles, which should be contracting (instead of your hamstrings, which should be relaxing). When your pedal reaches the seven o'clock position, think of driving the knee up toward the handlebar.

To use the hamstrings to generate power effectively and rest them when appropriate, remember these keys:

1. Feel the power created in the top half of the pedal stroke.

2. Begin the downstroke early, pushing down diagonally from 12 o'clock toward 4 o'clock.

3. When the pedal reaches the 3 o'clock position, initiate the backstroke. Try to pull the heel directly backward through the bottom bracket. This will not actually happen, but the attempt will encourage the optimal stroke.

4. When the pedal reaches the 7 o'clock position, pull upward and forward with the knee. Concentrate on using the hip-flexor muscles, located in the front-hip and upper-thigh area, and relax the hamstrings during this part of the pedal stroke.

Think about these technique keys on some of your rides. Learn to use the hamstrings during the pedal stroke phases in which they effectively deliver power and relax them on the others. You will ride faster late in races and definitely run faster off the bike.

Exercise Physiologist Ken Mierke is head coach of Fitness Concepts (www.Fitness-Concepts.com) and Director of Training for Joe Friel's Ultrafit.

Pedaling Drills

Pedaling economy can be improved by working on it a little during every ride. Do pedaling drills during your warm-up and cool-down on each ride. Pedaling drills are also great workouts to do on the trainer during the base training period and when it is too cold or dark to go outside.

One of the best workouts to increase pedaling economy is isolated leg training. See workout S1aL in the Chapter 12 workout menus for a full workout description. This is a drill that must be done on a stationary trainer. Rest one leg on a chair placed beside the trainer while your opposite leg does the pedaling by itself. Concentrate on eliminating any dead spots in your pedal stroke. Dead spots are indicated by clunking sounds made as you lose and regain pressure on the chain. CompTrainers have a feature called SpinScan. When you are pedaling in this mode you have a visual display on the screen that shows how much work each leg is doing.

My favorite efficiency workout is mountain biking. A mashing style breaks the rear wheel loose in most off-road terrain and gets you nowhere fast. Research at the Olympic Training Center has found that out of all of the cycling disciplines, mountain biking produces the most economical pedalers. USA Triathlon requires its junior team members to bring a mountain bike to spring training camps for this reason. Head off road for a fun way to improve your pedaling economy.

PEDALING TECHNIQUE SAMPLE WORKOUT

Warm up for 10 minutes with easy spinning.

Maximum Cadence Set 10 x 1 minutes as 10 seconds maximum cadence and 50 seconds easy spin recovery. Heart rate stays Zone 2 and below.

Spin-Up Set 8 x 2 minutes as 1 minute high cadence, 1 minute easy spin. Heart rate stays Zone 2 and below.

Single-Leg Set 8 x 3 minutes as 1 minute right leg only at 90 rpm, 1 minute left leg only at 90 rpm, and 1 minute both legs at 95 rpm. Heart rate stays Zone 2 and below.

10 minutes easy cool down.

PEDALING TIPS

- **Relax. Relax. Relax.** Do a total body inventory, and work on relaxing any muscles that are not contributing to your forward momentum. Wiggle your fingers and toes to check if they are relaxed.

- **Pedal horizontally.** Don't think about the pedal stroke as being up and down or even circular. Think of it as horizontal. At the top of the pedal stroke, think about pushing your toes into the front of your shoes before pushing down. At the bottom of the pedal stroke, think about pulling back and then up, as if you are scraping dirt off the bottom of your shoe. On the upstroke, think about throwing your knee over the handlebars.

- **Heel up.** Keep your heel slightly above the pedal during the entire pedal stroke. This effectively "rotates" the crankset forward and sets you up for horizontal pedaling, which is more economical than pedaling with a lot of motion at the ankle.

- **Unweight the pedal on the upstroke,** but don't pull it up.

Cadence

A low cadence requires a high force to be applied to the pedals. This is fatiguing for the leg muscles. A higher cadence at the same speed is more taxing for the cardiovascular system but less fatiguing to the leg muscles. This is a very important concept for triathletes competing in all distances. There is no costlier mistake for triathletes to make on the bike leg than pushing low gears hard to go fast. Coming off the bike with fatigued legs means trouble on the run. A higher cadence and a smooth pedal stroke allow a triathlete to keep going longer and keeps leg muscles fresh for the run.

A recent study completed at Colorado State University demonstrated that triathletes who pedal with high cadences will run faster off the bike. They theorized that this is due to a rhythm being established on the bike that produces an efficient running style immediately, with little bike-to-run transition time. With training, you can increase your cadence and maintain high speeds while keeping your legs fresh.

Cadence drills

Working a little bit on cadence every day is the best way to improve. Cadence drills are also great workouts to do on the trainer. Triathletes generally pedal at 70 to 80 rpm). Increasing cadence to 90 to 100 rpm is an acceptable goal.

Spin-ups. Slowly increase your pedaling cadence over 30 seconds to the maximum cadence you can hold smoothly without bouncing in your saddle. Recover by pedaling easily for several minutes and then repeat.

Downhill spins. Instead of coasting the descents when you are out riding, use them to practice your cadence skills. As you pick up speed on a descent, pick up your leg speed without shifting gears. Pedal as fast as you can to "keep up." When you hear a clunking sound (that occurs when you lose tension on the chain) or start bouncing in the saddle, shift up a gear to "catch up."

Granny-gear sprints. On a flat section of road, shift into your smallest gear and pedal smoothly and as fast as you can for 30 seconds. Recover and repeat.

CADENCE TIPS

- Pedal as smoothly as you can while you are increasing your cadence.

- Avoid rocking your hips and bouncing in the saddle.

- Relax every muscle, even the ones needed for pedaling.

- Pedal smoothly through the entire pedal circle, focusing over the top and back through the bottom.

- Keep your torso steady and let your legs do the work.

- Pedal from the hips.

- Think, "Smooth is fast."

Ankling

Ankling is excessive motion in the ankle during the pedal stroke. At the top of the pedal stroke, the foot is in a toe-down position, and the heel generally drops during the down stroke. At the bottom of the pedal stroke, the foot is in a heel-up position, and on the upstroke the heel comes up. Excessive ankling has been shown to be a waste of energy.

The most economical ankle position is to maintain a slightly toe-down (heel-up) foot position throughout the entire pedal circle. In recent years, Lance Armstrong has been a perfect model for this technique, and his race results show it.

BIKE-HANDLING SKILLS

Bike-handling skills all come down to how much speed you can safely carry. Obviously, applying the brakes less on a downhill or through a corner will mean reaching the finish line faster—unless you crash or go off course. Bike-handling skills are of prime importance for all types of triathlons but especially in off-road racing. You can conserve energy and move faster through technical terrain with good handling skills. An excellent book covering specific off-road riding technique is *Mountain Bike Like a Champion* by Ned Overend.

Improving your bike-handling skills on any course can mean taking minutes off your finish time. On a one-mile descent, increasing your speed from 25 mph to 30 mph will save you 24 seconds.

Shifting

Constantly monitor your pedaling cadence, and shift gears as soon as it moves out of your optimal range. Shift often, especially on off-road terrain. To ensure a quick, smooth shift, momentarily ease up on the pedal pressure as you shift. This eases chain tension and allows the chain to jump freely to the next gear.

Braking

Look ahead to anticipate when you will need to brake. Braking at the last minute allows you to carry a higher speed longer, but it requires practice and skill. Learn to read the terrain so you can brake at the last minute, but avoid locking up your wheels and causing them to slide. Wet and loose road and trail conditions require that riders take more care and leave themselves more braking time.

Cornering

Visualize a smooth arc on the ground around a corner, and follow that with your wheels. I visualize a thick red line on the ground exactly where I want to ride, and then I follow that line. Once you have picked your line, coast smoothly through it without any wobbles or major changes. The fastest line around a corner has the shallowest arc. This is the line that you will be able to safely carry the most speed. To ride the shallowest arc, enter the corner in the middle of the road. At the apex of the corner, move to the inside edge of the road, and then move back to the center after the turn.

Body position is very important to fast cornering, especially on downhill corners. On a left turn, your right foot is your outside foot. Your outside pedal should be down near 6 o'clock and inside pedal near 12 o'clock. Press your right inner thigh against your seat to lean your bike into the turn. Bring your chest down toward your stem to lower your center of gravity. Apply both your front and rear brakes to slow you down before the turn. Once you are in the turn, it is best not to apply the brakes. Applying the front brake will make your bike track in a straight line and resist turning. Applying too much rear brake in a turn will make your rear wheel lose traction and slide. Be even more cautious with your speed in loose and wet conditions. Once you have passed the apex of a turn, you can bring your bike to a more upright position and start pedaling. It is possible to power out of turns with more speed than you entered. Practice cornering in a traffic-free area. On a winding course, cornering fast will give you a big advantage over competitors who navigate turns more slowly. Some off-road courses have more than a hundred corners. Gaining one second per corner over your competitors means they have to use their fitness to catch up with you on the straight sections.

Downhill Riding

The fastest downhill position is low and streamlined, with your hands in the aerobars and your pedals parallel to the ground. However, this is not the *safest* position, due to decreased stability, low visibility, and lack of access to your brake levers. Practice will help you become comfortable and safe when descending on your aerobars. Practice moving from your aerobars to your brake handles, starting slowly and gradually adding speed. Remember that the faster your speed, the farther ahead you need to look.

When you apply the brakes, do so smoothly. Alternatively, sit up and let wind resistance slow you down. This technique has the added advantage of giving your body a refreshing break from the aero position.

During long-distance events, descents are a good time to do some stretching on the bike. When you are moving fast enough to be spun out in your largest gear, continue to pedal slowly. This will keep the blood circulating in your leg muscles, promote recovery, and help you to stay warm on long descents.

DOES YOUR BIKE DO THE SHIMMY?

Does your bike take on a life of its own on fast descents and start to wiggle around underneath you? Occasionally a bike will start to shake violently from side to side with increased speed. This is frightening, and unless you regain control, it can also be disastrous. There are several possible causes for a shimmy. On tall, lightweight frames with stiff, carbon-fiber forks, the top tube can twist out of alignment after hitting a bump in the road. The top tube then springs back, causing a shimmy. Rider position can also cause a bike to shimmy. A rider may be perfectly balanced over the bike in the aero position, but when this rider sits up or stands, his or her body weight shifts backwards. This lifts weight off of the front wheel, making it less stable and more susceptible to wobbling. To cure this wobble, the rider can shift weight forward, regaining balance over the wheels. A front wheel that is out of dish (meaning the rim is not centered over the hub) can also cause a bike to shimmy. A fork that is out of alignment could be the culprit as well. It is important to determine the cause of your shimmy, and to remedy the situation as soon as possible!

Uphill Riding

On a bike, climbing is all about making decisions. You must choose your gear and cadence, determine whether to pedal seated or standing, and decide to spin up a hill or power over it. Whether you are racing or training, the type of hill and your strengths and weaknesses will all factor into your decisions. During a race, you should choose the fastest way to get up the hill without causing undue fatigue to your leg muscles. In training, you may want to cause muscle fatigue to make your legs stronger.

On long, steady hills with slight grades, you should stay on the aerobars. As the grade gets steeper, the advantage of being in the aero position is reduced due to the lower speeds and wind resistance. This is a good time to sit up, slide back in the saddle, and use different muscle groups. Ride the hill seated, at a steady pace, with a medium to high cadence. Standing up out of the saddle and pedaling takes more energy than sitting, so limit the amount of standing you do.

On short, steep hills, you can use momentum to your advantage. Approach the hill with good speed. As the hill gets steeper and your cadence starts to drop, stand up and power over the hill without changing gears.

Rollers are a set of short hills, one after another. They can be incredibly fatiguing if you ride them like short, steep hills and power over each one of them. Rollers are the most technical types of hills, requiring attention to gearing and cadence at all times for optimal efficiency and speed.

To ride rollers efficiently, you must approach them like a long, steady hill. Stay in the saddle and spin up the hill with a medium to high cadence. Shift gears as the grade levels at the crest of the hill, maintaining a medium to high cadence, and accelerate over the crest of the hill. Most cyclists lose a lot of time by easing off over the crest. Once on the downhill, coast or shift down and pedal with a medium to low cadence. Stay in the saddle as much as possible to save your legs.

MOUNTAIN BIKE SKILLS

All triathletes will benefit from adding mountain biking to their off-season training. As mentioned beforehand, it is a powerful way to improve pedaling efficiency. Getting away from the traffic and into the woods is fun at any time of the year. Mountain biking will maintain the cycling muscles, increase bike handling skills, and keep your mind fresh and eager to ride your tri-bike when the race season rolls around. Improved bike-handling skills will increase your speed, confidence, and safety in technical race situations. Off-road triathlons such as the Xterra series events are a blast. Those athletes with good mountain bike skills have a significant advantage in Xterra races. With a few easily learned bike-handling skills, you can adventure into the dirt.

Balance

Balance is the first skill to perfect in order to mountain bike successfully—it is the foundation on which all mountain bike technical skills are built. Perfect balance is required before you can use your leg strength to power the pedals. Fitness is useless without balance. Weight distribution over the bike and center of gravity combine to create balance.

To have ideal balance, your center of gravity should fall at a point on the ground halfway between your front and rear wheel. On flat terrain, that should be achieved with your normal seated riding position—given a good bike fit. Visualize a flashlight tied on a string, dangling from the front of your waist. Where the light shines on the ground is where your center of gravity falls. When the terrain heads uphill, your center of gravity will fall back over the rear wheel. This requires you to move your center of gravity forward to retain balance. Neglecting to weight-shift forward when going uphill creates a very light front end, and your front wheel will lift off the ground or become light and wobbly, causing you to lose traction. You will subsequently become too unbalanced to power the pedals, lose momentum, have to stop riding, and put a foot down. Conversely, when the terrain heads downhill, your center of gravity will fall forward (visualize where your flashlight is shining), and the rear end of your bike will become lightweight. You must move your weight back to retain balance between your two wheels. Without a rearward weight shift on a downhill, your rear wheel may lift up high enough to flip you over the handlebars—ugh!

Balance lesson

Face a partner with your hands raised and your palms touching hers. Both partners stand on one leg and keep that leg straight. Using palms only (no thumbs!), knock your partner off balance. Repeat this lesson, but this time put your feet heel to toe, and then open them 10 inches wide (how your feet would look in the pedals at 3 and 9 o'clock). Bend your knees and lower your center of gravity. Now try to knock each other off balance. When did you feel the most stable? What was the difference between the two positions? How does that translate to mountain biking? Did lowering your center of gravity change anything?

How to weight shift

How do you shift your weight forward and rearward on the bike? Several different methods are possible. The common points to the different methods are to keep your core strong, arms and legs bent and supple, and whenever possible, lower your center of gravity by bringing your torso down toward your frame. To weight-shift forward, you can remain seated or stand up out of the saddle. Scoot to the front of your saddle, or, if standing, hover over the front end of the saddle and pull your sternum (breast bone) down toward your stem. Keep your elbows tucked in and low. To shift your weight back, you must raise your butt slightly out of the saddle and move your hips back. Remember to lower your center of gravity by lowering your torso down toward the frame as you move your hips back. Lowering your torso also allows you to keep your arms bent and reach the handlebars—a must for steering. As the grade of the downhill becomes steeper, you must shift your weight farther back and lower your center of gravity more. At the extreme position, your hips can be so far back and down that the saddle is at your navel, and the rear tire will buzz your butt. If you try this, be sure to keep your arms bent. I doubt that in this position it is possible to fly over the handlebars.

Practice these positions initially on flat, nontechnical ground in a traffic free area. See how flexible you can be and how far you can move around your bike. It is very hard to get back far enough to buzz your butt on the rear tire, but give that a go—you might like it!

Lateral balance and weight distribution

Beginner riders can mistakenly feel safer riding technical terrain by coasting with one pedal close to the ground in the 6 and 12 o'clock position, because it is more convenient for a quick bailout. One problem this creates is a low-slung pedal, which is likely to hit rocks and throw the rider off balance. The biggest problem, however, is uneven lateral weight distribution.

Let's examine this scenario: When 100 percent of a rider's body weight is supported on a single pedal, the bike will lean over to that side. A leaning bike turns to that side. To stay on the trail, rolling in a straight line, the bike needs to come upright. This can be done by leaning the upper body to the opposite side as a counterbalance. Wow, that sounds difficult! Add some challenging terrain, and it can quickly get overwhelming.

All these problems can be avoided by distributing your weight evenly on both sides of the bike with 50 percent body weight on each pedal and each hand. A clue I give to beginners is "Keep your weight on both feet." That means the pedals should be kept at approximately 3 and 9 o'clock when coasting.

The Ready Position

The ready position is the position to assume on your bike prior to any technical riding move. You must learn to be comfortable in the ready position. It is the most stable position and the base position from which all other technical skills progress. Perfect this in nontechnical terrain first.

- Weight distribution even between both feet
- Weight distribution even between both hands

PHOTO 4.1 *Rider in the ready position prior to tackling an obstacle.*

- Center of gravity lowered by bending arms and legs
- Butt off the saddle, but only by an inch or two
- Eyes six seconds ahead on the trail
- Core strong, arms and legs supple

Three Times and You're Out

When mountain biking, you can mindlessly pound out the miles, or you can consciously be aware of improving your skill. Use the "three times and you're out" rule every time you are riding a trail you find very challenging. On a section of trail you did not ride or could do better on, the rule is that you are allowed to try it three times only and no more. After three failed attempts, move on; otherwise you are drilling failure into your system. After the third unsuccessful try, you will be imprinting poor technique into your neuromuscular pathways and creating a mental blockage in your head (i.e., freaking yourself out). Move on and come back fresh another day.

If you approach a section and are not sure how to ride it or the best line to pick, get off your bike and push it through the section prior to attempting to ride. As you push it, feel how smoothly the wheels roll over the ground, check to see the chainrings do not hit any obstacles, and observe the steepest angle the bike reaches going over a drop-off. Ask yourself, "Is this something I can do? What techniques do I need to use to ride smoothly over this terrain?"

If you fail a technical section twice, close your eyes and visualize yourself riding perfectly through the section a couple of times before your third and last attempt. If possible, watch another rider complete the section before you try again. Challenge yourself, but back off anything you are uncomfortable with. Save it for another day.

Relax on Your Bike

To be a successful and fast mountain biker, you must train your body to be relaxed while riding over all types of terrain and at all intensities. You must learn to pedal smoothly at 90 rpm over bumpy terrain. Bumpy terrain can eventually "feel" as smooth as pavement when you are relaxed and efficient (honestly, this is true!). As with any sport, performing while relaxed is much more energy-efficient than while tense. To be most efficient at any sport skill, you must teach your body which muscles can be fully relaxed and which muscles need to be active at any time during a movement sequence pattern. For example, watch the facial muscles of 100-meter sprinters during a top-level competition such as the Olympics. Their jaws are so slack they wobble side to side with their stride. Meanwhile, their quads and other "running" muscles are working at maximum capacity. Mountain bikers need to have a strong and active core controlling balance and supple arms and legs to absorb bumps.

Mountain Bike Technique Drills
Relaxation drill

Initially you must have conscious awareness of which muscles are "mistakenly" tense and consciously relax them. Once you have repeated this awareness-conscious relaxation cycle several times, the correct movement patterns become unconscious and can be triggered by a key word or action.

To do the relaxation drill, set your watch to beep every minute during an off-road ride. Each time your watch beeps, do a total body inventory from head to toe and relax all nonriding muscles. Do this at different speeds and over different terrain each time. Relax your face, tongue, neck, and shoulders. Keep your core strong and active and arms and legs supple. When you do this, link it with an external cue. External cues can be words such as "strong core, supple legs" or actions such as inhaling and exhaling deeply or wiggling your fingers. (The latter one is what I use. It is so ingrained I can use it to relax at my desk, while driving, and while being annoyed by my four-year-old son). Repeat your external cue on every minute. Your external cue will become your "channel" to correct form. In a racing situation, you can say or do your cue to trigger perfect form unconsciously and get into the flow. The important part is to relax muscles selectively. Relaxing every muscle will turn you into a noodle, and you will lose control of your bike—not a good idea!

Pause drill

While riding along, remain seated in the saddle with both feet in the pedals. Apply the brakes and bring your bike to a full stop. Hold silently with no wobbling, pause for as long as you can remain in silent control, and then smoothly start pedaling again, proceeding forward in a straight line. Repeat the drill, but this time stand up out of the saddle.

Tip: Contract your abdominal muscles to aid with balance during your pause. Gradually work up to longer pauses.

Vision drill

While riding on singletrack, continually scan up and down the trail, but keep your eyes focused six seconds ahead. To get a feel for how far ahead six seconds actually is, count the seconds it takes for your front wheel to pass a tree or other object that is in front of you.

DRAFTING

Drafting is riding closely behind another rider, capitalizing on the windbreak he or she creates. It takes 30 to 40 percent (depending on your speed and wind direction) less effort to ride in another cyclist's draft than it does to ride alone. Sitting in another rider's draft can benefit you in two ways: It may enable you to ride faster than you can alone, and it may allow you to rest while maintaining your speed.

Drafting on the bike leg is allowed in professional ITU races and most overseas amateur triathlons. Drafting is also allowed in age group and professional Xterra races and in most other off-road triathlons. If you are entered in a race that allows drafting, you can use the technique to your advantage.

Drafting requires practice, as you need to get your front wheel within inches of the leader's rear wheel. One of the drawbacks of drafting is that your vision is blocked by the leading rider, reducing your ability to anticipate obstacles and dangers. You also risk touching your front wheel to the leader's rear wheel. The follower always comes off worse in this scenario. Drafting without touching tires or overlapping wheels takes practice.

The best way to learn to draft is to ride in a traffic-free area with one other cyclist. Make sure the lead cyclist knows you are learning to draft and rides smoothly and predictably. Start with a comfortable following distance, and gradually reduce it to a few inches. If there is a crosswind, the draft will not be directly behind the leader but a little to the side. Find the wind shadow created by the leader and move into that space. Again, be very careful not to overlap wheels when you are riding to the side of the leader.

When you are riding in a group, be conscious of others drafting you. Ride smoothly and predictably, and don't make sudden changes such as sharp braking or swerving. Point out obstacles, such as potholes or road debris, that a drafter will not be able to see.

RACING

At the start line I know all the money's in the bank and now I get to do some spending.

—Nicole Newton, professional triathlete

Do you crumble on race day or produce your finest performances? All the training in the world will not show an improved performance unless you can put it together on race day. Some riders "win" in training but then are consistently beaten at the races by a training partner they consider weaker. There is nothing more frustrating than underperforming on race day and ending up with a result you do not feel reflects your true potential. Race day execution is required for race day performance. There are few tricks and secrets to flawless race day execution, but it does take some thought, practice, and organization to get it right.

Pre-race Preparation

Many aspects of racing should be prepared, practiced, and perfected during training. These aspects involve decisions and actions you have control over. Pre-race preparations include the following:

- Correct training taper
- Race day equipment choice
- Pre-race meal
- Warmup routine
- Race pacing
- Race nutrition, hydration and electrolyte replenishment strategy
- Learning the course
- Knowing where the aid stations are and what will be available
- Learning the rules of the race
- Knowing the race start time

There are no excuses for making preparation mistakes. Spending three hours riding the course the day before an event will take the snap out of your legs on race day and is a stupid preparation mistake. Leaving your bike shoes at home and racing the bike leg in your running shoes is a preparation mistake. Don't put yourself in the position of say-ing, "I knew better than to _____." Perfect your preparation details in training until they are second nature and become a ritual. Repeating a pre-race ritual will give you confidence that you are perfectly prepared to race each time you toe the start line. Minimize the chance things will go wrong by becoming educated about the course, the race rules, making sure your equipment is in top condition, and you have arrived at the event with everything you need. Using a pre-race checklist helps immensely (see sidebar).

Dealing with Race Adversity

Triathlons are run in the great outdoors in far from controlled and sterile conditions. Many things can pop up to throw a wrench in your perfect race plan. How you deal with this adversity can dictate your race

PRE-RACE CHECKLIST

Race Essentials

Sense of humor and adventure

Tri-suit

Energy drink

Energy bars or gels

Post-race recovery drink

USA Triathlon license and identification

Race number

Heart rate monitor

Swim

Tri-suit

Wet suit

Goggles

Defogger

Skin lubricant

Bike

Bike

Helmet

Sunglasses

Shoes

Pump

Spare tools

Water bottles or hydration backpack

Run

Shoes

Cap or sun visor

Race belt

Fuel best

Transition

Bright towel

outcome and post-race satisfaction. A race can still be won after a flat tire or a wrong turn. When things go awry, you have two choices: to vent and throw your bike into the nearest field, or to focus on the specific tasks you need to complete to get back into the race quickly. Practicing unexpected situations in training gives you the tools to deal with them correctly in a race situation when your adrenaline is pumping. When you have a problem, focus on what you can control and how you can fix the problem, not on what you can't control— the race outcome. Practice repairing every mechanical problem that could occur on your bike, and learn the fastest way to do it.

On the Start Line

The air is thick with tension on every start line. Just thinking about the start of a race will increase your heart rate. Even the best-prepared athlete has some start line anxiety. It is important to realize this is part of the game and be comfortable with it. Out-of-control start line anxiety or bad start line habits can undermine your performance before the gun has even been fired. Pre-race excuses are one of the biggest start line no-no's. Here are my top 10 pre-race excuses:

- I didn't eat my favorite pancake breakfast.
- I haven't recovered from the last race.
- I had the flu all week.
- I am not used to my new bike, tires, shoes etc.
- I forgot my heart rate monitor and can't race without it.
- It is too cold/hot/windy/early/late for me.
- I have _____ injury (fill in the blank).
- I have tight hamstrings, quads, calves, etc.
- I didn't sleep last night.
- I haven't really been doing any training at all!

Vocalize, Visualize, and Believe

What you vocalize is what you visualize in your mind. What you visualize in your mind usually becomes true. If you believe the excuse you have made, your competitor has you beaten before the gun fires. Even if you don't believe the excuse you have made, you have planted a seed of doubt in your own mind that may take root later in the race when you are suffering.

HAS A FLAT TIRE EVER RUINED YOUR RACE OR EVEN SEASON?

Bill trained hard all year. His training went well and he reached his peak event, Ironman® USA, in the top physical shape of his life. He had practiced and perfected his nutrition and hydration plan. He knew precisely what heart rate to hold throughout the event to finish with a personal best time under 11 hours 30 minutes. His swim went as planned. Halfway through the bike his front tire went flat. One hour later he received assistance from race support to fix it, and he was on his way—one hour behind schedule and with no hope of a personal best. Oh well! Next year.

You spend many hours training. How about adding a few hours learning how to fix your bike and then practicing those skills? With a little practice it is very reasonable to fix a flat tire in under two minutes. In most races you can lose two minutes on the bike and still be in contention to win.

Get the right equipment, learn the moves, make a plan, and practice.

The equipment: A spare tube, tire levers, and CO_2 quick fill cartridges are the basics. Optional extras are a pump and a patch kit for that dreaded second
or third flat tire.

The moves: Take off your wheel. For the front wheel, open the quick release, undo the brakes, and the wheel should drop out of the fork. The rear wheel can be a bit trickier. A tight chain makes it difficult to remove the rear wheel. Make sure your chain is slack in the small front chain ring and smallest rear cog so the rear wheel slips easily out of the frame.

Remove only one side of the tire from the rim and extract the flat tube.

Check the inside of the tire for sharp objects that caused the flat. If any are still there, you must remove them before inserting the new tube.

Put the tire back on with your fingers only. The big danger with using tire levers for this job is pinching a hole in your new tube as you lever the tire back on the rim.

Use a CO_2 cartridge to inflate the tire quickly. Make sure the valve on your tube is open, the tire is seated on the rim properly and the tube is not pinched between the tire, and the rim before you inflate.

The training drill to fix a flat in less than two minutes

Phshsssssssss . . . oh no, a flat tire!

If it is a rear flat, before you stop riding, shift into your small chain ring and smallest rear cog (easiest combination for wheel removal).

Grab your new tube, open the valve, and start blowing it up with your mouth.

Remove the wheel.

Remove the tire from the rim on one side only.

Remove the flat tube.

Check the inside of the tire for sharp objects with your hand, and at the same time inspect the outside of the tire visually. Remove anything sharp.

Put the new tube into the tire (which now should be half inflated by your mouth).

Press the tire back onto the rim.

Make sure that the tube is not pinched between the tire and the rim.

Inflate with CO_2 cartridge.

Replace wheel.

Hook up brakes.

Spin wheel to make sure brakes are not rubbing and that wheel is straight in frame.

Hop on and get back into the race.

The time lost should be under 2 minutes.

The sudden stop after a flat tire can be a shock to your legs. When you get back in the race, give your legs a minute or two to warm up before you put the hammer down to make up the lost time.

It is unlikely anybody else is listening to what you have to say on the start line. However, if somebody does, he will see you as weak and have you already beaten in his mind. This is powerful and destructive stuff that you can observe on *every* start line.

Do you know somebody who is a regular pre-race excuse user? Are you? Listen carefully to yourself during your warm-up and at the start line. Every time a pre-race excuse pops into your head, replace it with a positive affirmation. If you want to blurt out, "It is too hot for me today," think "I love the heat" And "I do better than most in the heat." Replace every negative and fearful thought with a positive, confident one.

Wes Hobson had a long and successful career as a professional triathlete. He said, "I honestly can't think I ever had an excuse going to a start line. My philosophy was that I had a set training plan. I tried to follow it. Even though things came up and I couldn't follow the plan to a T, I am [at the start line] and I am going to do the best that I can."

Be positive, be confident, and, most important, have fun.

Transitions

Newbie triathletes generally regard the transition area as a place to rest and regroup—a place to celebrate the completion of one leg of the race and prepare for the next. Sometimes, it feels like the gravity in transition areas is ten times normal with food, drink, sunscreen, and friendly volunteers happy to chat. Out on the racecourse, everybody is pushing forward in the same direction. But in the transition area, athletes are milling around in all directions, and the sense of racing can disappear.

How many hours of swim practice would it take to lop two minutes off your swim time? Probably hundreds, maybe even thousands. How many hours of transition practice would it take to lop two minutes off your transition time? Maybe only one! Many triathletes are so focused on swim, bike, and run splits, they forget the clock is still running in the transition area. Every second counts. Transition practice isn't as fun as running, but it is a good investment of your training time. Triathletes looking to win need to shift their entire mental focus and integrate the transition seamlessly into their race. The transition is not a rest area but a place to speed in and out of, in the fastest time and with the least amount of energy.

Practice your plan: Write out a plan detailing exactly what you are going to do in the transition area, and practice it over and over again until you are fast with no mistakes. Practice it physically many times over in training, and then rehearse it mentally several times on race morning. By the time you are in the transition area during a race, you should be moving on autopilot. You can establish an edge on most of your competitors because most triathletes rarely practice transitions. Once you have a fluid plan perfected, simply repeat it on race day. Never try something new on race day.

PHOTO 4.2 *Running with your bike.*

Set up a clean transition stall: The fewer tasks you have to do in the transition area, the faster you will go. Keep your transition plan as simple as possible. Skip the socks and get rid of anything you don't absolutely need. Clutter will slow you down. Hang your bike on the transition rack by the seat and set your helmet on your handlebars upside down with straps open to the side. Nestle your sunglasses open in the helmet ready to put on quickly. Place as little stuff as possible on the ground. Bending down costs both time and energy.

Run with your bike: The distance from rack to mount line can be considerable at large triathlons. By running safely and quickly with your bike, it is easy to fly over this distance. Run upright with good form on the left side of your bike, holding your seat with your right hand (see Photo 4.2). The left side of your bike is the nondrive side (the side without the chain). Running on this side of your bike is safer as it keeps your legs away from the potentially skin-slashing chain and chainrings. Your left arm should be free in a compact running arm swing. Hold the bike upright to go straight and lean it to the side to turn. Practice running with your bike in a traffic-free area.

Bike shoes in the pedals: Coasting down the course at 15 mph while you put your feet in your shoes will move you far ahead of your buddy sitting on his butt in T1 doing the same task. Set your bike up in the transition area with your shoes attached to the pedals and rubber bands looped between the heels and frame to hold them horizontal (see Photos 4.3 and 4.4). Positioning your shoes in this manner will stop them from dragging along the ground while you are running your bike and minimize the chance that your shoe will hit something

PHOTO 4.3, 4.4 *Thin rubber bands hold the shoes in correct position.*

and come unclipped. Losing a shoe in the transition area will definitely slow you down. Also, the shoes are much easier to find when you start pedaling with your bare feet if they are positioned correctly.

On leaving T1, pedal with your feet on top of your shoes—the rubber bands will snap free on the first pedal revolution. Once you are cruising at speed, coast and slip your feet into your shoes. Keep your eyes ahead on the road at all times, not down on your feet. Slower riders, dropped water bottles, hats, and other various articles are common on the ground in a race transition area, and you don't want to run over any of these items.

On the return, slip your feet out of your shoes before you reach T2. Learn this skill first sitting in a chair or on an indoor trainer before taking it out on the open road (see Photo 4.5).

Speed over the mount/dismount line: Use a cyclo-cross mount and dismount (see sidebar on page 81) to cruise in and out of the transition area without losing any momentum. In the race, you will be doing this in bare feet, but initially learn and practice this skill wearing running shoes.

PHOTO 4.5 *Slip your foot into your shoe using one hand only.*

Attach your stuff to your bike: Handling small items sucks up time. Everything you need on the bike course should be attached to your bike. Tape gels to the frame; water bottles should already be on board, sunglasses looped to a cable, spare tube in a seat pack, and CO_2 cartridge taped to the seat post.

One outfit for all occasions: Start the swim with your full bike/run outfit under your wetsuit. A one-piece tri-suit is ideal. Anytime you change you clothes, it will add lots of time.

Navigation: Have you ever come out of a different mall door and had trouble finding your car? You can have a similar experience in a transition area. Note where your rack spot is and how to find it from the swim exit and bike entrance. From your rack, know where the bike and run exits are and the quickest route to them. Walk through the transition area prior to your warm-up, tracing the routes you plan to travel during the race.

Baby powder or Vaseline: To help your feet slide smoothly into your shoes, prime them with a sprinkling of baby powder or Vaseline.

Retain focus: Concentrate on yourself and not the spectators. I once coached an athlete who stubbed and broke his toe on the swim exit at an ironman while waving to his wife and son. He finished the race. He is tough. You are best to ignore the cheering crowds and maintain your focus for a fast and flawless transition.

Sample transition practice session

- Wearing your running shoes, run with your bike around a traffic-free area for a few minutes. Practice left and right turns and different speeds. Get comfortable with it.

- Wearing your running shoes, run with your bike, hop on, pedal for 30 seconds, then hop off, run with your bike for 30 seconds, and then hop on again. Repeat four times.

- Set your bike up on a stationary trainer with your shoes attached to the pedals. Practice pedaling with your feet on top of your shoes and putting on and taking off your shoes with one hand. Don't look at your feet. Keep your eyes focused on the road ahead.

CYCLO-CROSS MOUNT/DISMOUNT

Learn and practice fluid mounts and dismounts without stopping to speed up your transitions on and off the bike. It is much faster and more energy efficient to run your bike over the mount / dismount line and hop on your bike from a run than it is to run over the line, come to a full stop, mount your bike, and then accelerate back up to speed. Pro triathletes seamlessly flow from running with their bikes to riding without a change in speed or momentum. You don't need to be a pro to do this. With a little practice you can have transitions just as fast as the pros.

Learn this technique wearing running shoes. In a triathlon you should be able to do this with bare feet.

Mount: Start by running with your bike (Photo 4.2). Remember to run on the non-drive side. Transfer both hands to the top of the handlebars (Photo 4.6). Leap your right foot off the ground and land on your

saddle with the inside of your right thigh (Photo 4.7). Slide down into your saddle and start pedaling.

Dismount: Slow your bike to a reasonable running speed. Transfer both hands to the top of your handlebars. Stand up out of the saddle. Swing your right leg over the back wheel (Photo 4.8), forward between

your frame and left leg and onto the ground (Photo 4.9). Hop your left foot off the pedal just before your right foot strikes the ground. Transfer your right hand to the saddle and bring your left arm into a run swing and transition seamlessly into running with your bike.

- Clip your bike shoes into the pedals (you are standing beside your bike in bare feet). Rotate the cranks to 3 and 9 o'clock position with your favorite side forward. Using thin rubber bands or dental floss, tie up your shoes parallel to the ground. Run with your bike to make sure your shoes are held firmly in place and don't drag on the ground. Repeat this until you have it perfect.

- Put it all together. Set up a transition area, mimicking race conditions. Run in with bare feet as if from the swim, put on your sunglasses and helmet, grab your bike, run it to the mount line, hop on, pedal up to speed with your feet on top of your shoes, slip your feet into your shoes, ride for a few minutes, remove your feet from your shoes, pedal in to the dismount line with your feet on top of your shoes, hop off your bike, run it to your stall, take off your helmet, put on your running shoes, and go. Repeat until you are flawless.

Race Tactics

Renowned road cycling coach Eddie Boryscwicz, commonly known as Eddie B, defines tactics as "anything you can do to help yourself succeed and your opponents not to succeed." Everything is a consideration: the course, the weather, your strengths and weaknesses, your competitors and their abilities, your energy intake, your warmup—anything that will affect your race outcome. Race tactics may allow an athlete with inferior fitness to win the race. Some athletes are notorious for "winning" in training but fail to produce good results on race day. The strongest athlete does not always win; sometimes the *smartest* one wins.

Tactics for nondrafting events

In nondrafting events, you are racing against the clock. Your fellow competitors do not have great influence on your race outcome. Most tactical decisions in nondrafting events should be made long before race day and perfected in training. The two most important decisions are pacing and refueling. Determine what speed you should ride to give you the fastest possible bike split and leave enough in your legs for a competitive run. You should always finish the bike leg knowing you could have ridden faster. The bike leg is the best leg for fuel intake, so decide where and when you will eat and drink.

Tactics for draft-legal events

In draft-legal events, you have an opportunity to use other competitors to your advantage. To do so, you need to know your own strengths and weaknesses and what use another competitor can be to you. Drafting is a major advantage for triathletes who are fast swimmers and slow cyclists. Once on the bike leg, the faster swimmer can jump on the wheel and into the draft of a passing slower swimmer/faster cyclist. The slower rider can then sit in the draft using less energy and keep up with the superior cyclist. (Yet another reason for those cyclists to get to the pool!)

Tactics for draft-legal off-road triathlons

Off-road triathlons add another dimension to tactical decision making. Off-road courses travel over paved roads, dirt roads, and singletrack and require a much wider variety of bike handling skills. Most Xterra triathlons use a mass start with all age groups in one wave. This means your tactical decisions and actions can involve athletes in different age groups. As in the swim, you can draft competitors in different age groups and use them to pull you up to the leaders in your age group. Let riders you are drafting know if you are not in their age group. It is then less likely they will attack and drop you from their draft—they don't need to waste the energy. If your age group leaders are not as smart as you are, you can keep on going right past them in the draft.

Pacing

Drafting is not the only way to take advantage of a superior cyclist. On singletrack and at slower speeds, when it is difficult and often ineffective to draft, pacing comes into play. Pacing is when you match the tempo of a stronger rider and stay on her wheel even though you may not be quite as strong. You can use a stronger climber to pace you up a hill. This is like having a carrot on a stick—a strong motivation to keep you going. You can descend faster by following the lines of a superior rider and keying off her smooth handling skills and increased speed.

On the flip side, watch out for weaker riders pacing you. Get rid of them by attacking and opening a gap. In singletrack, this gap needs only to be as far as the next corner. Once you have established enough daylight between you and your pacer, settle back into your rhythm.

The short burst of extra energy you expend to remove a pacer may get you to the run start minutes ahead. Don't lose sight of the fact that you need to leave enough energy in your legs for the run. The winner is the first athlete across the finish line, not the first off the bike.

Know the course

Knowing the course is a significant advantage in off-road events. The best thing to do is to pre-ride the course, but if you do not have time, get as detailed a description of it as you can. When pre-riding a course, the important things to notice are available passing areas, places where the singletrack starts and ends, and places that are less technical, where you can eat and drink. Also look for sections that are likely to have a headwind, making drafting an advantage. Practice riding through the technical sections and determine the fastest line. If you are not sure how to ride a section, watch a few other riders and then copy the one who looked the smoothest. Usually the smoothest rider is the fastest.

Know your competition

Knowing the strengths and weaknesses of your fellow competitors is essential in order to take full advantage of them. You can get an idea of a rider's skill with some careful observations. Is the rider pedaling smoothly with a high cadence? Riding in a straight line? Wasting energy in any way? If a rider looks sloppy, there is a good chance that rider will be a poor bike handler and hold you up in the singletrack. It would be to your advantage to sit in his draft on the road, conserving your energy, and then to use a little extra effort to pass before the singletrack starts.

If in doubt, aim to be first into the singletrack. You may create a gap over a rider who is less at home in technical singletrack, or you will hold a superior rider back—both are to your advantage. The only time you should let a rider reach the singletrack in front of you is when you are sure you can take advantage by pacing him.

Passing

Good sportsmanship and judgment are important when you are holding a rider back in the singletrack. If riders are not in your age group, you must let them pass as soon as it is safe. The fastest way to get around another rider in the singletrack is to be polite and ask. If you are rude, many riders will not move over as quickly as they might have done otherwise. You do not need to let riders in your age group pass. Beating them to the singletrack and blocking them may be a good tactic. This is infuriating if you are the rider being blocked—but that's racing.

Working together

When you are riding head to head with another athlete in your age group, you have two choices: You can try to get ahead of him by attacking, or you can work together. Two riders working together will always be faster than one lone rider. Two riders can trade off drafting and resting. The stronger climber can take the lead uphill, and the stronger descender can take the lead downhill. Both riders can avoid power surges, as they will not have to race each other to the singletrack and attack to drop each other. Too many power surges are draining and can leave you with dead legs for the run. If you are a stronger runner, it is to your advantage to work with another rider during the bike leg.

C H A P T E R

5 Exercise Physiology

xercise physiology is the science of how the body responds and adapts to exercise. Understanding exercise physiology will allow you to think your way through a smart training plan rather than just blindly follow something from a magazine. To become the best athlete you can be, you need to know your own body inside and out. Everyone will respond to the same exercise stimulus in a slightly different way depending upon factors including genetics, aerobic training base, muscle strength, age, sex, nutrition, and the ability to recover. With these elements in mind, you can analyze and learn the ways in which your own body responds to exercise and develop the optimal training plan for you. When you are in tune with your body, you can identify your strengths and weaknesses, where they come from, and what to do to improve them. In essence, you will become your own scientist.

There are eleven principle physiological systems in the human body: integumentary (skin, hair, nails), skeletal, muscular, nervous, endocrine, cardiovascular, lymphatic, respiratory, digestive, urinary, and reproductive. Each of these systems must be functioning properly for peak athletic performance, but the four most important to an athlete in training are the nervous, muscular, cardiovascular, and respiratory systems. These are the elements that make up your engine, and understanding them will help you train your engine properly.

THE HUMAN ENGINE

Nervous System

The nervous system consists of your brain, spinal cord, and nerves. Its function is to perceive and respond to internal and external events. Finely tuning the correct muscle-sequence firing pattern for efficient pedaling, being able to relax on the bike at 50 mph, and deciding what pace to push in a race are some of the jobs the nervous system does for us while we are cycling. Chapter 4 was devoted to training the nervous system through skills, techniques, and tactics.

Cardiovascular System

The cardiovascular system consists of the heart, blood vessels, and blood. Your heart is your fuel pump. It pumps blood to your lungs, muscles, and the rest of your body. Triathletes love to compare their heart rates. This is a meaningless exercise; if your resting heart rate is 10 beats per minute lower than your buddy's, it does not mean you are fitter or faster than he is. You should know your own heart rate information so that you can compare your current data to your previous data. A decrease of ten beats per minute in your resting heart rate over a period of six months indicates increased fitness. Your heart is stronger and can pump the amount of blood your body requires at rest with fewer beats per minute.

The major role of your blood, as far as exercise is concerned, is to bring glycogen and oxygen to the working muscles and to remove metabolic waste products. Oxygen is carried by hemoglobin found on the red blood cells. The volume of your blood that is made up of red blood cells is known as the hematocrit level. One of the physiological benefits of aerobic training is that it stimulates an increase in the production of red blood cells and thus increases the oxygen-carrying capacity of the blood.

Respiratory System

The respiratory system consists of the lungs and airways. The lungs are where the exchange of carbon dioxide and oxygen between the air and blood takes place. The respiratory system seldom limits performance unless an athlete suffers from a problem such as asthma or a respiratory illness.

Athletes will detect two key ventilation benchmarks when increasing the intensity of their exercise. The first is the initial deepening of the breath; this is the aerobic threshold (AeT). The next benchmark is the point at which breathing becomes labored, the breath feels like it changes from breathing to sucking, and there is an audible increase in the ventilation rate. This is the ventilation threshold (VT). In laboratory settings, VT is always closely related to lactate threshold (LT). VT can be used as a reliable and noninvasive field test to estimate LT.

Muscular System

Skeletal muscles exert a force on the skeleton to bring about movement. Muscles are attached to the skeleton by tendons. Muscles that decrease joint angles are called flexors, while muscles that increase joint angles are called extensors. The quadriceps are hip flexors, as they decrease the joint angle at the hip when they contract. The quadriceps are also knee extensors, as they increase the joint angle at the knee when they contract.

One muscle is made up of many muscle fibers. There are three types of skeletal muscle fibers: fast-twitch type IIa, fast-twitch type IIb, and slow-twitch type I. Each of these three types of fibers have both anaerobic and aerobic capabilities. The slow-twitch fibers are predominantly aerobic and the fast-twitch fibers are predominantly anaerobic. Fiber type is determined by the nerve to which the muscle is attached (so it cannot be changed with training), and fiber-type percentage is genetically influenced. Successful power sprinters generally possess a high percentage of fast-twitch fibers, whereas endurance athletes generally possess a high percentage of slow-twitch fibers.

TABLE **5.1** MUSCLE FIBER CHARACTERISTICS			
PROPERTY	TYPE I SLOW-TWITCH	TYPE II A FAST-TWITCH	TYPE II B FAST-TWITCH
Energy system	aerobic	combination	anaerobic
Resistance to fatigue	high	high/moderate	low
Speed of contraction	low	high/moderate	highest
Blood supply	high	high	low

The capability of the existing fibers can be enhanced with training, however. Aerobic workouts will improve the aerobic capabilities of fast-twitch muscle fibers, giving them the properties of slow-twitch fibers. Type IIa muscle fibers are interesting, as they can take on the characteristics of either type I or type IIb muscle fibers depending on the predominant style of an athlete's physical training.

Physiology will help you determine exactly what is limiting your athletic performance. Ask yourself the following questions after a race or hard workout: What was my limiter? What was holding me back? Why couldn't I go faster? Select from the following four answers:

- My heart
- My lungs
- My legs (muscles)
- My head (mental aspect)

Did you have to slow down because your heart was pounding in your chest? Were you unable to get enough oxygen into your lungs to enable you to go faster? Perhaps your heart rate was low and your breath was controlled but your legs just wouldn't turn. Maybe you were just were unmotivated to ride hard. The answers to these questions will tell you much about the direction your training needs to take in order for your performance to improve.

ENERGY SOURCES FOR CYCLING

Adenosine tri-phosphate (ATP) is the source of energy used by all muscle cells for force production. ATP is available only in small amounts and must be constantly replenished. Your body has three ways of creating ATP. These three energy systems are the aerobic energy system, the lactic acid system, and the creatine phosphate system. All three systems are at work constantly, but depending on the duration and intensity of the exercise being performed, one system will predominate. Each energy system has advantages and disadvantages. Specific training can target one of these three energy systems and strengthen it over the others.

Aerobic Energy System

Triathlons are primarily aerobic events, and triathletes should focus the bulk of their training on the aerobic energy system. (Beginner and long-distance athletes should focus *heavily* on the aerobic energy system.) The aerobic energy system does the lion's share of energy production when the body is at rest or exercising at an easy to moderate pace. The aerobic energy system uses oxygen and muscle glycogen as its predominant fuel source and will also use fat as a fuel source during exercise bouts that last more than 20 minutes. The aerobic energy system can also use protein as a fuel source in very small amounts. The waste products of this energy system are carbon dioxide and water—both excreted easily by the body.

The main characteristic of the aerobic energy system is its dependence on the availability of oxygen. As exercise intensity increases, so does the demand for oxygen. There comes a point when the body reaches a limit in the speed at which it can deliver oxygen to the working muscles. This is called the maximum aerobic capacity—in physiologist's shorthand, VO_2max. Though the term VO_2max is bandied around on training rides, it is often misunderstood.

The aerobic energy system is closely tied to the cardiovascular and respiratory systems. Specific physiological adaptations the body makes to aerobic training include the following:

- Increasing the ability of the heart to pump blood
- Increasing the ability of the blood to carry oxygen
- Increasing the ability of the working muscles to extract oxygen from the blood
- Increasing the number of capillaries supplying the working muscles with blood
- Increasing the activity of aerobic enzymes
- Increasing the number of mitochondria (intracellular organelles that are the sites of metabolic reactions in the aerobic energy system)

The aerobic energy system uses a long sequence of chemical reactions to change glycogen or fat into ATP, making it a slow producer of ATP during exercise. The advantages of the aerobic energy system are that fuel sources are virtually unlimited and waste products are easily excreted.

Lactic Acid Energy System

As exercise intensity increases, the lactic acid energy system becomes a more predominant energy producer. This system is anaerobic and uses muscle glycogen as a fuel source in the absence of oxygen to produce ATP. The waste product of this process is lactic acid, which is not easy for the human body to excrete and causes problems when it builds up in any amount. The lactic acid energy system can produce ATP rapidly, but the limit to this system is the amount of lactic acid the body can tolerate. Normal, resting lactic acid level in the blood is about 1milliMole. Once lactic acid rises above a certain level, metabolic functions are affected.

Lactic acid is comprised of two parts, the lactate molecule and the hydrogen ion (H+). The hydrogen ion creates an acidic environment in the muscles. This reduces the activity of key enzymes and interferes with the ability of muscles to produce force. The lactate molecule can be used as an energy source by the aerobic energy system. Lactate is transported out of the muscle cells and into the blood.

Lactate level in the blood is a balance between the amount being produced by working muscles and the amount being removed and metabolized by other tissues. As the muscles work harder, there comes a point at which lactic acid is produced faster than it is removed. This point is called the lactate threshold. Physiologists' shorthand term for lactate threshold is LT—another common term discussed on training rides.

At and above the lactate threshold, muscles become bathed in an acidic environment and muscle-fiber contraction is inhibited. This is the point at which your legs start to feel heavy and slow. It is the point at which you start to think "this feels hard." It is the point when your ventilation changes from breathing to sucking.

From a physiological standpoint, aerobic capacity (VO_2max) and lactate threshold (LT) are two important measures of your fitness for triathlon racing. The higher your lactate threshold as a percentage of VO_2max, the faster you will ride for an extended period of time. Lactate threshold is highly trainable and is an important element for all short-course athletes and elite long-course athletes to improve. Chapters 8–10 will explain how to train lactate threshold and other abilities for peak performance.

Creatine Phosphate Energy Producing System

The creatine phosphate energy producing system is also an anaerobic system. Of the three energy systems, it is the fastest producer of

ATP. While it can produce ATP almost instantly, the energy will be depleted in 5 to 10 seconds. Creatine phosphate is an important energy system for sprinters to develop, but it is not an ability used in triathlon racing.

C H A P T E R

6 Training Principles

Knowing the principles of training is as important as knowing your own physiology. What stimulus do you need to give your body in order to produce gains in athletic performance? Understanding the principles of training will help you design a training plan that is perfect for you and only you. The basic principle of training is this: When you give your body a certain stimulus (overload) and then allow it to rest, the body will supercompensate and become stronger. Dr. Tudor Bompa defines training adaptation as the "sum of transformations brought about by systematically repeating exercise."

SIX TRAINING PRINCIPLES

The changes the body makes in response to exercise are not random occurrences, but follow proven training principles. There are six training principles we must keep in mind when designing an effective training program: overload, adaptation, load progression, specificity, individuality, and reversibility.

Overload

Overload occurs during training and is defined as anything that will challenge your current state of fitness. Overload may go to very challenging levels but should never pass the point of injury. The magnitude of a load is a combination of the workout duration and intensity.

Adaptation

Adaptation occurs during rest. Rest and recovery are often the most overlooked aspects of a training plan. Athletes who have no rest programmed into their training plan do not allow adaptation to occur, limiting the ability to improve their fitness. These athletes become increasingly fatigued with training and eventually succumb to illness, injury, and burnout. Do not let this happen to you! Taking rest days and weeks is as important as physical training.

Load Progression

The overload you apply must be gradually increased over weeks, months, and years to produce a training stimulus. Once your fitness has increased to a certain level, the stimulus producing that level will no longer be challenging. Doing the same workout week after week will cause you to plateau and feel stale. You must continually but gradually raise the applied overload for improved performances. Raising the overload too quickly will not allow your body to adapt, increasing the likelihood of injury. On a more subtle level, you may not be training the intended ability. For instance, you may have a goal to increase aerobic endurance. From exercise testing you know that cruising along with a heart rate of 120 beats per minute puts you in your aerobic training zone. Then you "raise the bar" too quickly with the mindset "more and faster is better." You start riding with a heart rate of 150 beats per minute, which may be your lactate threshold. Instead of developing your aerobic endurance, you are developing your lactate threshold, which was not your original goal.

Specificity

The abilities you train and the overload you apply determine what adaptations your body will make. Doing bicep curls at the gym will make your biceps stronger but will not improve your 40k cycling time trial. Playing tennis every day may be fun but will not decrease your bike splits. If your goal race has a flat course, you will be best served by spending the bulk of your training time on flat terrain. If one of your limiters is endurance, you will improve more quickly by doing long rides at a steady aerobic pace than by sprint training. You need to determine what abilities are needed for your goal race(s) and specifically train them. The stresses applied in training must be similar to the stresses found in your goal events.

Individuality

Each athlete has different training needs and athletic abilities. Age, cycling experience, capacity for work, health, recovery rate, body build, nervous system, training time, nutrition, and psychology are variables for everyone. You may follow a training plan from a successful athlete and find that it does not produce any performance gains for you. In fact, following somebody else's training plan is like running in somebody else's shoes—they do not fit right and are likely to leave you injured. It is important to individualize your training plan to fit each one of your unique needs and abilities.

Reversibility

If you stop training, you will lose your fitness. Swimmers have been shown to have a 10- to 15-percent decline in their aerobic capacity after only one week out of the water. This means you must be mindful when you resume training after a layoff and start at a lower level than you were training immediately before you stopped. Account for the length of time you spent off the bike, and whether injuries or illness kept you out of the saddle, before you jump back into your training routine.

REST AND RECOVERY

Webster's dictionary defines recovery as "the regaining of something that has been lost or taken away." No amount of training will do you any benefit—and in fact may do you harm—without sufficient rest and recovery. This is the most abused and ignored training principle. You can't train a tired body. Athletes should use every method available to speed and enhance their recovery from workouts. Using scientifically proven recovery techniques can reduce your fatigue level and quickly get you back to feeling good and riding fast. The faster you recover from a workout or race, the sooner you can do another workout or race, and the more high-quality training you can do. This pattern will improve your athletic performance and development over time. Quality training time is extremely valuable. By "quality" I mean that you are fully recovered and capable of complete focus and effort. These sessions should be spent wisely.

The following is a common scenario among athletes: Bob, a hard-working and highly motivated athlete, feels flat, and his race times are slow. He figures that he must somehow be losing fitness or not trying

SYMPTOMS OF OVERTRAINING

Physical Indicators

- Decreased performance times
- Weight loss
- Slower recovery in heart rate after exertion
- Abnormal rise in heart rate on standing
- Increased resting heart rate
- Sluggish, heavy legs
- Persistent muscle soreness
- Swollen lymph glands
- Loss of menstruation in women
- Increased incidence of infections, allergies, injury, headaches
- Diarrhea

Emotional indicators

- Loss of motivation
- Apathy toward races and results, desire to quit during competition
- Trouble sleeping, flat, tired, depressed, and lethargic
- Irritable, unable to relax
- Loss of appetite
- Decreased libido

hard enough, so he trains harder. It is more likely that Bob needs to rest and unload an accumulation of fatigue. Bob's scenario is a classic downward spiral. As he trains harder, and loads more fatigue into his body, he will find his race times slipping further, so he will train even harder. Finally, a deep state of fatigue, an illness, or an injury will stop Bob and force him to take a break. This state of deep fatigue is known as overtraining, and recovery can take weeks, months, or even years.

Don't risk making the same mistakes in your training. It is far healthier to be undertrained than to be slightly overtrained. There is a fine line between overtraining and peak performance when you are seeking to do your best, and you must be careful when you are walking on that line. Incorporating recovery techniques into your daily life will reduce your risk of overtraining.

Training and recovery are the yin and yang of athletic performance. One has no benefit without the other. Over-reaching is required to stimulate your body to adapt. Full recovery is required to allow that adaptation to take place. Partial or no recovery leads to partial adaptation, lack of performance gains, and eventually overtraining. Regardless of what you do, when you extend yourself, your body requires a specific amount of time to refuel and repair. Full recovery takes time.

Training + Recovery = Adaptation

Training + Inadequate Recovery = Performance reduction,
Illness, Injury, Burnout

No training + Recovery = Detraining

Active Rest versus Passive Rest

Passive rest is complete rest with no activity at all. Active rest is a short, very light ride to "spin out the legs" without added fatigue. To decide whether active rest or passive rest is more appropriate, you must determine your fatigue level. If you are struggling to get off the sofa, a complete day of passive rest is in order. At this level of fatigue, even a very easy ride will produce additional fatigue in your legs. If you are highly motivated to ride but do have tired legs, a short, easy recovery ride may be to your benefit. An easy spin for an hour or less can reopen the 30-minute recovery period, giving you an additional opportunity to replenish muscle glycogen.

Sleep

Sleep is vital for recovery. Sleep time is when your body does its best repairing and rebuilding. Skimp on sleep and you will delay recovery. One of the biggest advantages professional athletes have over age groupers with full-time jobs is they are able to sleep 10-plus hours a night and nap in the afternoon. Through the course of a night, you cycle through several sleep phases. During the slow-wave stage, growth hormone is released by the pituitary gland stimulating tissue repair. To improve recovery:

- Get eight hours of sleep per night.
- Ingrain a routine. Go to bed and rise at the same time every day of the week, even on the weekends.
- Take a 45-minute nap in the afternoon if you have the time available.

Daily Nutrition Habits

The health status of your body and the amount of training you can withstand and adapt to is dictated by your daily nutrition habits. What you eat and drink sets your athletic potential. If you eat poorly on a daily basis, your potential will be low. Ultrafit coach Tom Rogers says, "You can wear yourself out with bad nutrition even faster than by exercise without discipline." Maintaining daily optimal health through a nutritious diet will do more to speed your recovery from workouts than any other factor.

Read *The Paleo Diet* by Loren Cordain for some no-nonsense information about what and how to eat for long-term health. The first step to improving your diet is to eliminate all processed foods. Get rid of the junk. Most of your calories should come from lean meats, seafood, fresh fruits, vegetables, and nuts. Make sure everything you put in your mouth has a high nutrient value. Other nutritional guidelines:

- Avoid eating and drinking empty calories.
- Avoid contaminating your system with synthetic foods and drinks such as sodas.
- Track your calorie intake to ensure you are taking in sufficient total calories per day to replace what you burn. Don't trust your appetite since fatigue can decrease appetite. A daily calorie deficit will leave you with low fuel stores and slow recovery. Even a small daily deficit added up over weeks and months can be debilitating and lead to injury and illness. Progressive glycogen depletion is the top cause of overtraining.
- Track your protein intake to ensure you are consuming a minimum of 0.6 grams of protein per pound of lean body mass per day. Increase this to 0.8 grams if you are training for three or more hours that day. www.fitday.com is a useful tool for tracking calorie and nutrient intake on a daily basis.
- Maintain proper hydration status by drinking enough water to pee clear once a day. If you are peeing clear once an hour you are over-hydrating.
- Keep your prescriptions current.
- Take a multi-vitamin, iron, and calcium if recommended by your doctor.
- Consider supplementing your diet with antioxidants, such as vitamins E and C.

Other Keys to Maxmizing Recovery

Time Management. A day spent running all over town, doing a month worth of errands, does not equal a recovery day. Poor time management can also eat into sleep hours. Identify time-wasting hours in your day. Do you watch TV? Spend hours surfing the internet? Activities like this can be relaxing but will slow your recovery if you sacrifice sleep for them.

Stress Management. Chronic stress causes illness, injury, and burn-out. Obviously these are not good things for athletic performance. Identify what your sources of stress are, and if possible, eliminate them. Design a strategy to manage the stress source if elimination is not possible. Some options are to increase your coping skills and recruit emotional support.

Yoga. Stretching, relaxation, and meditation all have been shown to speed recovery. Practice a method of yoga, such as Hatha yoga, which focuses on balance, flexibility, and meditation.

Massage. Massage speeds recovery by increasing circulation, flushing away waste products, and bringing in fresh nutrients. It also feels so good and promotes relaxation. Visit a certified massage therapist for a professional massage. Use a foam roller or tennis ball to self-massage daily.

Cold Therapy. Cold therapy can speed recovery by increasing blood flow, raising the level of oxygen, and increasing metabolism.

RECOVERY TECHNIQUES FOR TRAINING

Many athletes allow time for recovery following big events, however, recovery techniques should be actively incorporated in your training program in order to be effective. Learn to prepare yourself properly for rides. Get in the habit of eating a meal containing carbohydrates and protein 2 to 2.5 hours before you ride. To combat dehydration and electrolyte imbalance, drink 6 to 8 ounces of a sports drink immediately before you begin a ride. Learn to eat and drink adequately during rides, and create a post-ride recovery ritual that you follow every time you get off the bike.

Recovery on the Bike

Proper fueling and hydrating during exercise will allow you to reach the end of a session in the best possible shape needing less time for total recovery. For easy workouts under one hour, a simple sports drink containing carbohydrates and electrolytes, such as Gatorade, will suffice. For rides longer than one hour, careful attention should be paid to hydration, electrolyte intake, and fueling to avoid depletion.

Hydration and electrolyte replacement. Your body's thirst drive depends on two things: an increase in blood salt concentration and a decrease in blood volume. Both of these things occur when you sweat. Research has shown your body will absorb and retain more fluid when electrolytes such as sodium are added to the beverage. Plain water dilutes the sodium in your blood and shuts off the thirst mechanism, causing you to drink less and risk dehydration. For a sports drink to be effective, it must contain at least 75 milligrams of sodium per 8 ounces of fluid. Research has also shown that a 6-percent carbohydrate solution is absorbed into the body faster than plain water. Aim to drink 8 ounces of fluid every 15 to 20 minutes, and adjust this volume based on heat and humidity. A drink with higher than a 6-percent carbohydrate solution will probably cause gastric distress.

Fueling. Athletes can burn over 900 calories per hour during exercise. However, research contends the maximum rate of carbohydrates that can be absorbed from the stomach and processed by the liver during exercise is one gram per minute. This is a measly 240 calories per hour, so replacing every calorie burned is an impossible task. Testing calorie intake on rides by trial and error is the only way to really dial in on your personal optimal level of calorie replacement. In general, the lower the intensity of the workout, the higher the calorie load your body can process. Direct athlete experience in this area does not align with the scientific research. Elite ironman triathlete Gordo Byrn reports personal cycling success with 600 calories per hour intake. Focus on replenishing only as many carbohydrates as your body can process. Consuming more than this will just leave you bloated.

Fuel choices. Exactly the right type of solid, semi-solid (gels), and liquid food combination to consume during exercise is highly personal. One athlete may thrive on bananas and Gatorade. This menu may send another athlete sprinting for the port-a-potty. Research shows adding protein to the workout beverage increases endurance performance and speeds recovery. However, protein is harder to digest and may cause gastrointestinal problems for some athletes. Again, use trial and error to figure out what works for you. It is vital to continually train with the fuel that you plan to consume in a race.

Post-Ride Recovery Techniques

The bulk of recovery techniques should be following after a ride. Hard training rides that last an hour or more put severe demands on your body. The four things you need to be aware of after long and hard rides are dehydration, electrolyte imbalance, glycogen depletion, and muscle damage. The job of post exercise nutrition is to regain hydration status, replenish electrolytes lost, replace carbohydrate burned, provide protein for muscle repair, and antioxidants to reduce cellular damage. Taking care of each of these details will speed your recovery.

During exercise your muscle cells take up glycogen at a higher rate than when at rest. At the end of an exercise bout, this effect lasts up to 30 minutes. Glut-4 molecules hang out on the muscle cell membrane and grab glucose from the blood. Glut-4 molecules are superactivated by high intracellular calcium and insulin levels produced during exercise. Refueling within 30 minutes of the end of an exercise bout enables you to take advantage of Glut-4s while they are still ramped-up. This will quickly replenish your muscle glycogen. If you miss this window, it can take up to 48 hours to fully replenish your muscle glycogen fuel stores. Refueling during this 30-minute window will speed up your recovery significantly. After you ride, start the refueling process immediately by drinking a recovery beverage. A liquid recovery meal is best during the 30-minute refueling window, particularly if you don't feel like eating after a long or hard ride.

Carbohydrates and protein. Your recovery drink should contain both carbohydrates and protein—a 4:1 ratio is ideal. The appropriate amount to consume is 0.5 grams of carbohydrate and 0.125 grams of protein per pound of body weight. Commercial products such as Endurox R4 contain these elements and have been shown to be superior to drinks with carbohydrates alone. Next, you should consume a meal 2 to 4 hours later to complete your recovery. This meal should be composed of 60 percent carbohydrates, 20 percent protein, and 20 percent fat.

Rehydrate. Weigh yourself before and after exercise. Drink 24 ounces of fluid to replace every pound lost. Choose from water or a sports drink. Avoid sodas and alcohol.

Antioxidants. A recovery drink should also contain antioxidants. Vitamin C and E have been shown to reduce free radical damage.

Branched chain amino acids. Include L-valine, L-leucine, and L-isoleucine in your recovery drink. These branched chain amino acids may decrease muscle breakdown, reduce central nervous system fatigue, and help maintain your immune system.

L-Glutamine. Immune system function is depressed after a race or hard training session. Another amino acid, L-glutamine, is a primary component in white blood cells. Supplementing with L-glutamine may enhance immune system function and may reduce the risk of illness during heavy training periods.

Remove heat stress. In hot climates, remove heat stress from your body immediately after your race finish. Most races finish near the swim start. Walk waist deep into the water and stay there for 5 minutes or until your body temperature feels normal. This will stop you from sweating, halting the dehydration process and loss of electrolytes.

Speedy recovery from training will be a key component in your performance over weeks and months of training and racing. Make the most of your recovery, and you will get the most from your training.

7 Measuring Intensity

Intensity is a rating of how hard you are working. It is the qualitative component of the work you do while riding your bike. The more work you do per unit of time, the higher the intensity of your workout.

Why measure intensity? How hard should you work when doing intervals? How easy should your recovery ride be? What pace can you maintain in a time trial? How fast can you ride and still run well off the bike? These are some of the reasons it is important to know your exercise intensity. If you ride hard every day, all you will achieve is chronic fatigue. The human body simply cannot handle that level of work. The best way to improve your performance is to modulate your training intensity and allow for recovery time.

Many of us have done stellar bike splits in a race and then expired on the run. If we knew what our optimal intensity was, we could have ridden fast and still had enough energy for a good run. There are several methods used to gauge exercise intensity on the bike. Perceived exertion (PE) is a subjective measure of how you feel. Speed is a measure of how fast you are going. Heart rate is a measure of how hard your cardiovascular system is working. Power output is a measure of how much power you are generating. Each of these measures gives us a view of what is going on during exercise; however no one method provides the complete picture, and each has pros and cons. Performance is a function of a wide range of variables. Interpreting these variables—heart rate, feel, power, pace, mood—is a key skill to learn and develop.

HEART RATE

An overwhelming majority of people who have heart rate monitors (HRM) just watch the numbers and think: "Cool, I reached 180 beats per minute in my workout today. Gee whiz!" Without specific exercise testing, the numbers you see on your heart rate monitor will be interesting, and perhaps fodder for boasting, but not particularly useful. To make your HRM into a useful gadget, you need to identify a key reference point that can be used to gauge your exercise intensity. This key reference point is your lactate threshold heart rate (LTHR). This is the point at which lactic acid in your blood begins to accumulate faster than it is removed. (See Chapter 5 for a more thorough description of lactate threshold.) Using LTHR as a landmark we calculate

MEASURING INTENSITY: PROS AND CONS

Speed

Pros. Measuring speed is inexpensive and simple with a handlebar cycling computer. Speed can be a good intensity measure under consistent conditions, such as indoors on a calibrated trainer.

Cons. Speed is affected by many external factors such as terrain, weather conditions, tire pressure, and equipment. Due to this variability, speed cannot be used as a reliable intensity gauge to guide and log your training.

Heart Rate

Pros. Heart rate has become the most popular method of measuring exercise intensity in recent years, in part due to the availability and reasonable costs of heart rate monitors. A heart rate monitor is portable and can easily be used on multiple bikes. Training methods based on heart rate have been firmly established and are relatively easy to follow.

Cons. Heart rate is an indirect measure of exercise intensity. It is a physiological response to exercise and has a time lag of approximately 40 seconds. This means that it takes about 40 seconds for your heart rate monitor to show how hard you are working. For short, high-intensity repetitions of less than 60 seconds, such as sprint and power training, heart rate is not a good indicator of exercise intensity. Heart rate is also affected by heat, humidity, dehydration, nervousness, excitement, and diet. Some athletes find the chest strap annoying and uncomfortable.

seven heart rate zones—Zones 1–5c. When you are exercising within each of these zones you are training a specific physiological system within your body.

Identifying Lactate Threshold

To get an accurate and true reading of your lactate threshold, you must perform a graded exercise test while having your blood drawn and analyzed for lactate at regular intervals. Athletes who do not have access or do not want to go to a testing facility can get a good estimate of their lactate threshold with a field test. A 30-minute, maximum-effort, evenly paced time trial can establish a relatively accurate estimate of lactate threshold. Identifying ventilation threshold with field testing will also give you a relatively accurate estimate of lactate threshold.

Power

Pros. Power provides an immediate and direct measure of exercise intensity. The moment you apply extra pressure to the pedals, the power meter records an increased power output. Power is therefore a more accurate gauge of exercise intensity than heart rate for short-duration intervals. Power does not have the subjective rating problems of perceived exertion and reflects the extra energy needed for wind and hills.

Cons. Power meters such as the Power-Tap and SRM are gaining popularity, although their high prices may put them out of the average cyclist's reach. Power meters are difficult to move between multiple bikes. Because reliable, on-bike power meters are a relatively recent luxury, effective training routines based on power production are difficult to find.

Perceived Exertion (PE)

Pros. Measuring your perceived exertion requires no equipment and is free. All you need is to be in tune with how hard your body is working.

Cons. PE is a subjective measure and is affected by many things. PE increases over the course of a workout even at a constant power output. Anything that affects your judgment will sway your PE. Mental preparedness, environmental conditions, stress, fatigue, excitement, and other riders will all affect your PE.

MAKING YOUR TESTS WORTHWHILE

Testing is a method of monitoring your training progress and establishing training zones. It is important to take care with the protocols you follow when testing yourself. You need to be clear on what exactly you are testing, what data you want from the test, and what kind of test is most appropriate for you. Your test must be reliable. If your methods change from test to test, you cannot compare the data. Make sure you repeat the test under exactly the same conditions as you completed it before. Use the same pre-race meal, warm-up, equipment, and course. Try to conduct outdoor tests when the wind is relatively calm and the temperature is warm. Arrive at each test well rested; testing when you are fatigued is a waste of time. Ease up and reduce training intensity and volume two days prior to the test. Never test just for the sake of testing. Know what information you need from the test and how you are going to use it to refine your training in the future.

Lactate threshold is the most important physiological determinant of cycling performance. The higher your lactate threshold is as a percentage of VO_2max, the faster you will ride for an extended period of time. The percentage of VO_2max is variable based on each individual and his or her state of training. One rider may be below LT riding at 90 percent of her VO_2max, whereas another rider may be deeply anaerobic and way above his LT at 90 percent of VO_2max. To ensure that you are training the physiological system you are targeting, you must reference your heart rate training zones to lactate threshold (see Table 7.1). With these heart rate training zones, you can design an effective training plan to maximize your potential.

Field test to estimate lactate threshold heart rate (LTHR)

For this test you will need a flat road where you can ride for at least 15 minutes without stopping. You will also need a heart rate monitor that will calculate your average heart rate. Make sure that you are well rested before you attempt the test. Record every detail related to your test so you can copy it exactly on the next test in order to produce consistent and comparable data. Use the Test Results Worksheet in Appendix C to record all relevant data. Before the test, warm up for at least 30 minutes and include a few hard efforts of 1 to 2 minutes. Do the test ride 15 minutes out and 15 minutes back on a flat course without stopping. Pacing is crucial to producing good, repeatable test results. You need to ride the 30-minute time trial as fast as you can and keep an even pace throughout the ride. If you "blow up" at any point during the trial, the test results will not be accurate. Record your average heart rate for the last 20 minutes of the 30-minute time trial; this is your estimated LTHR. Also record the weather conditions, how you felt, and your average speed for the time trial. Keep this information in a training journal, as it will be valuable to compare this data to results from future tests.

TABLE **7.1**   CROSS-REFERENCING HEART RATE ZONES AND LACTATE THRESHOLD

ZONE	PURPOSE	% OF LTHR
1	Recovery	65–81
2	Aerobic	82–88
3	Tempo	89–93
4	Sub-threshold	94–100
5a	Super-threshold	100–102
5b	Aerobic capacity	103–105
5c	Anaerobic capacity	106+

OTHER HEART RATE REFERENCE POINTS
Resting Heart Rate (RHR)

The lowest number you will see on your heart rate monitor is your resting heart rate (RHR). This is useful to record on a daily basis. This number will drop (to a point) as you become more fit. A rise in this number can be an indicator of illness, overtraining, or detraining. The best time to record your RHR is first thing in the morning before you get out of bed. To do this, simply take a pulse count at your wrist. Be consistent and record your RHR at the same time and in the same way every day. When your RHR jumps more than 5 beats per minute in a 24-hour period, it is a warning sign that you may be getting ill or are

TABLE 7.2 HEART RATE ZONES

Find your lactate threshold heart rate (bold) in the "ZONE 5a" column. Then read across left and right for training zones.

ZONE 1 RECOVERY	ZONE 2 EXTENSIVE ENDURANCE	ZONE 3 INTENSIVE ENDURANCE	ZONE 4 SUB– THRESHOLD	ZONE 5A SUPER– THRESHOLD	ZONE 5B ANAEROBIC ENDURANCE	ZONE 5C POWER
90–108	109–122	123–128	129–136	**137–140**	141–145	146–150
91–109	110–123	124–129	130–137	**138–141**	142–146	147–151
91–109	110–124	125–130	131–138	**139–142**	143–147	148–152
92–110	111–125	126–130	131–139	**140–143**	144–147	148–153
92–111	112–125	126–131	132–140	**141–144**	145–148	149–154
93–112	113–126	127–132	133–141	**142–145**	146–149	150–155
94–112	113–127	128–133	134–142	**143–145**	146–150	151–156
94–113	114–128	129–134	135–143	**144–147**	148–151	152–157
95–114	115–129	130–135	136–144	**145–148**	149–152	153–158
95–115	116–130	131–136	137–145	**146–149**	150–154	155–159
97–116	117–131	132–137	138–146	**147–150**	151–155	156–161
97–117	118–132	133–138	139–147	**148–151**	152–156	157–162
98–118	119–133	134–139	140–148	**149–152**	153–157	158–163
98–119	120–134	135–140	141–149	**150–153**	154–158	159–164
99–120	121–134	135–141	142–150	**151–154**	155–159	160–165
100–121	122–135	136–142	143–151	**152–155**	156–160	161–166
100–122	123–136	137–142	143–152	**153–156**	157–161	162–167
101–123	124–137	138–143	144–153	**154–157**	158–162	163–168
101–124	125–138	139–144	145–154	**155–158**	159–163	164–169
102–125	126–138	139–145	146–155	**156–159**	160–164	165–170
103–126	127–140	141–146	147–156	**157–160**	161–165	166–171
104–127	128–141	142–147	148–157	**158–161**	162–167	168–173
104–128	129–142	143–148	149–158	**159–162**	163–168	169–174
105–129	130–143	144–148	149–159	**160–163**	164–169	170–175
106–129	130–143	144–150	151–160	**161–164**	165–170	171–176
106–130	131–144	145–151	152–161	**162–165**	166–171	172–177
107–131	132–145	146–152	153–162	**163–166**	167–172	173–178
107–132	133–146	147–153	154–163	**164–167**	168–173	174–179
108–133	134–147	148–154	155–164	**165–168**	169–174	175–180

TABLE 7.2 HEART RATE ZONES (CONTINUED)

ZONE 1 RECOVERY	ZONE 2 EXTENSIVE ENDURANCE	ZONE 3 INTENSIVE ENDURANCE	ZONE 4 SUB-THRESHOLD	ZONE 5A SUPER-THRESHOLD	ZONE 5B ANAEROBIC ENDURANCE	ZONE 5C POWER
109–134	135–148	149–154	155–165	**166–169**	170–175	176–181
109–135	136–149	150–155	156–166	**167–170**	171–176	177–182
110–136	137–150	151–156	157–167	**168–171**	172–177	178–183
111–137	138–151	152–157	158–168	**169–172**	173–178	179–185
112–138	139–151	152–158	159–169	**170–173**	174–179	180–186
112–139	140–152	153–160	161–170	**171–174**	175–180	181–187
113–140	141–153	154–160	161–171	**172–175**	176–181	182–188
113–141	142–154	155–161	162–172	**173–176**	177–182	183–189
114–142	143–155	156–162	163–173	**174–177**	178–183	184–190
115–143	144–156	157–163	164–174	**175–178**	179–184	185–191
115–144	145–157	158–164	165–175	**176–179**	180–185	186–192
116–145	146–158	159–165	166–176	**177–180**	181–186	187–193
116–146	147–159	160–166	167–177	**178–181**	182–187	188–194
117–147	148–160	161–166	167–178	**179–182**	183 188	189–195
118–148	149–160	161–167	168–179	**180–183**	184–190	191–197
119–149	150–161	162–168	169–180	**181–184**	185–191	192–198
119–150	151–162	163–170	171–181	**182–185**	186–192	193–199
120–151	152–163	164–171	172–182	**183–186**	187–193	194–200
121–152	153–164	165–172	173–183	**184–187**	188–194	195–201
121–153	154–165	166–172	173–184	**185–188**	189–195	196–202
122–154	155–166	167–173	174–185	**186–189**	190–196	197–203
122–155	156–167	168–174	175–186	**187–190**	191–197	198–204
123–156	157–168	169–175	176–187	**188–191**	192–198	199–205
124–157	158–169	170–176	177–188	**189–192**	193–199	200–206
124–158	159–170	171–177	178–189	**190–193**	194–200	201–207
125–159	160–170	171–178	179–190	**191–194**	195–201	202–208
125–160	161–171	172–178	179–191	**192–195**	196–202	203–209
126–161	162–172	173–179	180–192	**193–196**	197–203	204–210
127–162	163–173	174–180	181–193	**194–197**	198–204	205–211
127–163	164–174	175–181	182–194	**195–198**	199–205	206–212

Source: *The Triathlete's Training Bible*, 2nd ed. by Joe Friel (Boulder, CO: VeloPress, 2004).

not recovered from your previous workouts. In this case you should examine yourself closely for other signs of illness or fatigue. When you have several warning signs, you should make the day's workout very easy or take a rest day. A gradual rise in RHR over a period of several weeks may be a sign that you are overtraining and need to schedule more rest into your training plan. Tracking your RHR every day helps you to identify and respond to these issues.

Maximum Heart Rate (MHR)

The highest number you will ever see on your heart rate monitor is your maximum heart rate (MHR). For the most part, this number is genetically determined and does not change significantly with training. MHR is not a good predictor of performance. Several formulas are available to help you estimate your MHR. The most commonly used equation is:

220 − age = MHR

The answer will be an estimate, however, and may not give you an accurate sense of your MHR. You can do some exercise testing to find your MHR; however, these are very strenuous tests and may not be appropriate for you.

LTHR, RHR, and MHR are your "own" numbers. No useful information can be gained by comparing your heart rates with someone else's numbers. However, comparing your own heart rate numbers with those from a previous date, along with other data such as PE, speed, and power output, can be informative. For example, if you rode 12 miles in 30 minutes with an average heart rate of 150 beats per minute on April 1, then you repeated the same exercise on July 1 but rode 12.5 miles in 30 minutes with the same average heart rate, you know you have increased your fitness.

POWER

Power, which is measured in watts, quantifies of the rate of work produced by a cyclist.

Power (watts) = work (joules) ÷ time (seconds)

Power (watts) = force (newtons) x distance (meters)

Power provides an immediate and direct measure of exercise—sometimes called the measure of truth. Heart rates can distort the "truth," as variables such as heat and humidity will elevate HR. Nothing

UNDERSTANDING HEART RATES

Heart rate numbers should be considered interesting information. You cannot draw conclusions about fitness or rest status solely from heart rate numbers. Doing so may cause you to make decisions about your training that are not based on solid evidence. Here are some things to keep in mind when considering your heart rate readings:

- There is no information to gain by comparing your heart rate to another athlete's.
- Resting heart rate rises when you are tired, sick, on the road to getting sick, and stressed.
- Resting heart rate can be lower than usual when you are over-trained.
- You are tired and need rest when your heart rate does not fall as far or as quickly as normal between intervals.
- You are tired and overreaching when your heart rate is higher than normal at a certain speed or power output.
- Attempting to reach a goal heart rate may send you into higher training zones than desired if you are tired.
- Heart rate will be higher with increased heat and humidity.
- Heart rate will be lower when it is colder.
- As altitude increases, so to does your heart rate.
- Caffeine and certain other stimulants will increase your resting and exercising heart rates.
- Your maximum heart rate is largely genetically determined and will not change with training status.
- The equation 220 − age = max HR is a poor estimate for most athletes—especially women and masters athletes who have been in race shape for many years.
- Heart rate can increase during a workout, though perceived exertion and watts may remain the same. This is called cardiac drift.
- It is possible to pick up another athlete's heart rate on your monitor.
- Overhead power lines can cause your heart rate monitor to show erratic readings.

will interfere with power measurements, however. If you do not put power into the pedals the numbers will not show up on the power meter. Power output provides instantaneous feedback with no time lag, and is therefore a more accurate gauge of exercise intensity than heart rate for short intervals. Power does not have the subjective rating problems of perceived exertion, and it reflects the extra energy needed for wind and hills. You can compare your power outputs to those of other cyclists, but remember that a heavier cyclist will need to produce more power than a lightweight cyclist to achieve the same speed when climbing. This effect is negligible on flat terrain.

Two ways to increase your power output on the bike are to shift to a harder gear while maintaining cadence (pedal harder) or to increase your cadence while remaining in the same gear (pedal faster). Power is directly related to performance. The more power you generate, the faster you will ride.

POWER TRAINING ZONES
Critical Power (CP)

For any given duration you have a critical power (CP). This is the maximum average power output that you can achieve over that duration. As the duration increases, your CP decreases. You can maintain higher

TABLE 7.3 CRITICAL POWER VALUES AND SYSTEM CHALLENGED

CRITICAL POWER	SYSTEM CHALLENGED
CP0.2	max power
CP1	anaerobic endurance
CP6	aerobic capacity
CP30	lactate threshold
CP60	aerobic endurance
CP90	aerobic endurance

average power outputs over 12 minutes than you can over 30 minutes. CP values can be used to guide your training intensity. The common CP values used are CP0.2, CP6, CP30, CP60, and CP90.

Field test to establish critical power values

CP can be accurately tested in the field without special equipment other than a power meter. Choose a flat course for all CP tests. Be sure to warm up and to follow the testing guidelines shown in the sidebar on page 106. To establish a certain CP level, do a time trial with an all-out effort for the duration of the CP value you are testing. Record your average power output for the time trial. Maintain a controlled, evenly paced, maximum effort over the duration of the time trial. You may have to try the test several times before you learn how to pace yourself optimally. This is good training for racing. If you "blow up" after riding 6 minutes of a 30-minute time trial, don't worry, all is not lost; you have just recorded a good CP6 value. If you finish the time trial with lots of energy in reserve, the average power recorded will not be a good reflection of your ability for that CP zone.

Computing CP60, CP90, and CP180. Testing for the longer duration CP values is strenuous and can be hard to fit into a training plan. Fortunately, you can predict the longer duration CP values from a CP30 value. As you double the duration of the CP value, reduce the average power output by 5 percent. For example, from a CP30 equal to 300 watts, you can predict a CP60 of 285 watts.

Establishing critical power training zones. CP values can be used to establish the following training zones: CP0.2, CP1, CP6, CP30, CP60, CP90 and CP180. To establish the training zones, add and subtract 5 percent from each CP value. For example, a CP30 of 300 watts will establish a CP30 training zone of 285 to 315 watts.

Calories per kilojoules. Your power meter will tell you exactly how many kilojoules of work you did on a particular ride. This number can be used to estimate the number of calories you burned on that ride. For example, 1000 kilojoules (kJ) = 240 Calories (kCal)

The average cyclist is 22-percent efficient, meaning that only 22 percent of the calories burned are used to put power into the pedals. A cyclist who has produced 1000kJ on a ride will have burned 1,091 calories. Roughly speaking, you can estimate you have burned 1 calorie for every kilojoules your power meter records. This information is useful for athletes monitoring their body composition, fueling during long events, and refueling for recovery after a ride.

Date CP30 and goal CP30. Date CP30 is the value obtained from your most recent test. Goal CP30 is the power output you need to maintain in order to reach the performance goals you have set for your next peak event. You can calculate your goal CP30 at www.analytic cyling.com or by analyzing power-output profiles from prior events. Your training can then be focused on specific numbers, as you know where you are and what you need to achieve.

PERCEIVED EXERTION

The goal in a race is (usually) to go as fast as you can. Heart rate monitors and power meters can actually hold you back in race circumstances. In races that have high status, such as world championships and the Olympics, an athlete's excitement and motivation level is much higher than in regular training. The increased adrenaline and stimulus leads to breakthrough performances, producing heart rates and power outputs never seen before—as well as world records. Athletes who ignore their PE and focus solely on the numbers produced by their power meter or heart rate monitor will hold themselves back from breakthrough performances. If you control your pacing strategy by how you feel, you leave the door open for a breakthrough performance.

However, PE can be imprecise and confusing given the extra motivation and circulating adrenalin on race day. It is easy to float through the first quarter of a race feeling great but going at a pace that is too fast

TABLE **7.4** PERCEIVED EXERTION AND EFFORT

PE	BREATHING LEVEL	EFFORT LEVEL
1–2	Hardly noticeable	very little
3–4	Slight	easy
5–6	Aware of a deepening of the breath	moderate
7	Starting to breathe hard	strong
8	Breathing hard	very strong
9	Heavy, labored breathing	extremely strong
10	Maximal exertion noted in breathing	maximal

to maintain. As the race duration increases, the importance of using a power meter or heart rate monitor as a governor to control your pace also increases. Pacing too fast in the first 40 miles of an ironman-distance bike leg will be very costly come the run and will significantly increase the effort needed to complete the race within your target time.

MULTI-SYSTEM TRAINING

You can take advantage of heart rate, power-output measurements, speed, and perceived exertion all together to get the clearest picture of your training condition and exercise intensity. Training is the most effective when multiple measures of intensity are concurrently monitored.

Power-pulse Training

The heart of triathlon training is muscular endurance. This is the ability to go fast at a steady pace for a long time. This is steady riding at slightly below your lactate threshold for short-course triathletes and further below lactate threshold, at about 65 percent of CP30, for ironman-distance triathletes. Combining power, heart rate, and PE into your training will allow you to finely focus your muscular endurance training. To do this, ride for as long as you can at your goal CP30 and finish the interval when your heart rate exceeds your LTHR plus 3 beats per minute.

Power-pulse workout

Warm up, then do a time trial at goal CP30 until your heart rate reaches LTHR plus 3 beats per minute. Spin easily for 25 percent of the work interval time, and then repeat this three times. Retest your date CP30 and set new goals when you have a work interval lasting 20 minutes or more. For example, during a workout such as this, your first interval may last 16 minutes followed by 4 minutes of rest, your second interval may last 12 minutes followed by 3 minutes of rest, and your third interval may last 9 minutes. Lower your goal CP30 if you cannot complete an interval of at least 6 minutes.

Power-pulse–PE Training

Including a "feel for it" with PE adds another level of insight to your training. If you find that the workout just described feels very easy, make a note of that in your training journal. The following week you may repeat the workout, manage to hit the same numbers on your monitoring gadgets, but find that it required much more of an effort. It took more out of you, meaning you had a higher PE. This indicates that something is going on with your body that needs attention. You may be fatigued, sick, dehydrated, or stressed. Ignoring these factors can be detrimental to your performance progress. Ideally, the same workout producing the same numbers will feel easier each time you repeat it.

PART THREE

The Training Plan

CHAPTER

8
Individualize Your Training Plan

Individuality is one of the six core principles of training discussed in Chapter 6. Individualizing your training plan means tailoring it to your personal abilities and to the demands of your chosen event. Following a plan designed exactly for you will bring you the most performance gain with the least amount of effort. Remember, following a plan designed for somebody else may take a lot of energy and produce little in the way of results, leaving you frustrated and doubting your athletic talent. This chapter will help you to design a training plan that is just right for you.

Begin by following these steps to find out what you really want and what is holding you back from getting it.

- Set goals
- Analyze your personal abilities
- Analyze your event demands
- Calculate your limiters

SET "SMART" GOALS

The first thing to determine is exactly what you want to achieve. What are your goals? Is this the year you are going to break one hour in the 40k time trial? Are you going to step up and complete an ironman-

GOALS AND DREAMS

There is a distinct difference between goals and dreams. Goals are stepping stones on the way to your dreams. To represent your nation at the Olympics is a lifetime achievement. If this is your first year racing, going to the Olympics is probably a dream not a goal. The key is to achieve a steady progression of increasingly challenging goals. Goals plot the course for your success. Eventually, what was once a dream may become an achievable goal.

distance event? Qualify for Hawaii? Are you going to set a personal best in the local Cold Lake Olympic Triathlon? Take time to think carefully and specifically about your goals, as they should form the core of your training plan.

Your goals must be clear, concise statements. They should motivate you and keep you going when you otherwise might give up. Goals will tell you where you need to go and how to get there, and they will show you when you are making progress. Here are some guidelines to follow when designing "SMART" goals.

Specific: Goals must be specific and easily understood. For example: "Finish a 40k time trial under an hour." If you set a general goal such as "get in shape," you will not reach a specific point of achievement.

Measurable: It is clear when you have achieved a measurable goal. For example, if your goal is to run 10 miles, when you have completed that run you have achieved your goal and can move on.

Attainable: Your goal must be challenging and hard to reach, but not impossible. If you set lofty goals, you will probably disregard or ignore them. Unrealistic goals will not motivate you either—and may discourage you instead. Don't confuse goals with dreams (see sidebar on this page). However, setting a goal that is too easy to achieve will not encourage you to strive for your personal best.

Relevant: The goal must be yours. It must be personal, relevant to you, and you need to be passionate about it. "Completing an ironman-distance triathlon before the age of 40" is a personal, motivating goal.

Time-bound: Goals must have specific parameters, such as a date for completion. For example: "Run 10 miles by May 31." In this scenario, you will have either achieved or not achieved your goal by May 31; it will not linger.

You should record your goals so you can periodically review them. Rereading your goals will keep them fresh in your mind. Some athletes tape their goals to their bathroom mirror so they see them daily.

Once you have a goal, you can start to make some smart choices to help you reach it. Analyze the demands of your goal event. What abilities are needed in order to succeed? There are six abilities available for an

A CLASSIC STORY OF GREED AND GOAL INFLATION

Even the most experienced athletes (me included) get greedy when they see performance gains—they want more. In 2000, after the birth of my son, I trained "gently" with steady running—nothing fancy—to get back in shape. Nine months after his birth, I ran a marathon with the goal of finishing and enjoying the experience. I finished in 3 hours and 33 minutes. I thought that was pretty good going considering I didn't put any effort into my training, so I decided the next year I would like to be faster. I sought more experienced training partners and ran with them. I met them at 5:30 a.m. at the track for intervals, I got faster, I started to beat them, and I started to get greedy. Now I not only wanted to run faster than last year, but I wanted to win my age group. I ran harder, faster, and longer, loving every minute of it. (I love a good, hard workout!) My goals inflated with every passing week and soon I thought I could be in the top 10 overall. I was good! I did a 17-mile training run with some of the local guys and was the only woman who had ever kept up with them. We hammered out 6:30- to 7:00-minute miles the entire run. The next day I could hardly walk, and after a week of forced rest I was still limping. My right knee had developed tendonitis with six weeks to go before the race. I frantically rehabbed my knee with icing, stretching, physical therapy, and more. After six weeks I was not limping anymore, but it took me four months to be able to run again and six months to run without pain. I was a spectator at the marathon and cheered my friends across the finish line. Hopefully I learned my lesson. As the saying goes, mechanics should never fix their own cars. Coaches should never coach themselves!

athlete to train. The first three are the foundation abilities: endurance, force (strength), and speed skills (see Figure 8.1). Every endurance athlete, regardless of the type of racing or distance of the event, must start by establishing a solid foundation with these three abilities.

THE FOUNDATION ABILITIES

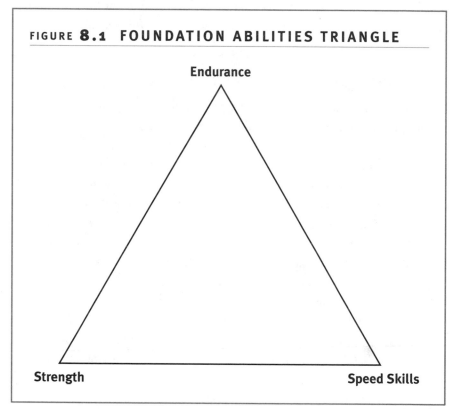

FIGURE **8.1**   **FOUNDATION ABILITIES TRIANGLE**

Endurance

Strength

Speed Skills

Endurance

Endurance is the ability to do something over and over again. It is the ability to keep going to the end of your event both physically and mentally. The duration of your event dictates the amount of endurance you need. A sprint-distance triathlon typically takes just over an hour. An Xterra off-road triathlon typically takes about three hours. The Xterra racer will thus need to put a greater emphasis on endurance training than the sprint-distance triathlete. Endurance is the first ability for beginners training for any distance triathlon to develop. It is the key ability for all triathletes competing in half- and full-ironman–distance events. Long, steady rides in heart rate Zone 1 to 2 or at 60 to 65 percent of CP30 develop aerobic endurance. See E1 and E2 workouts in the workout menu in Chapter 12.

Strength

Muscular strength is the maximum force that a muscle or muscle group can generate. Increased strength will help you when you have to push down hard on the pedals, such as up steep hills and into headwinds. If your event is likely to have headwinds or is hilly, it will be important to emphasize force work in your training plan. Strength can be developed by lifting weights, riding hills, riding into headwinds and riding seated in a big gear. See F workouts in the workout menu.

Speed Skills (Technique)

Speed skills encompass every technique that you can practice and perfect in order to go farther and faster using less fuel. They are so important that I devoted Chapter 4 of this book to developing the techniques, skills, and tactics used in riding and racing. Off-road courses are more technical than road courses; therefore off-road triathletes should place even more emphasis on skills work in their training plans.

Once a solid base of the three foundation abilities has been established, the advanced abilities can be trained. The three advanced abilities are muscular endurance, anaerobic endurance, and power (see Figure 8.2). Each of these abilities is a combination and refinement of the foundation abilities.

ADVANCED ABILITIES
Muscular Endurance

Muscular endurance is the ability to make repeated contractions against a submaximal load. It is a combination of strength and endurance, and it is essential to keeping the pedals turning over against a high load for a long period of time. Muscular endurance is an important ability for sprint- to half- ironman–distance triathletes. Elite ironman athletes also need to train muscular endurance. Age-group ironman triathletes, however, should emphasize aerobic endurance and do only a small amount of muscular endurance work. See the M workouts in the workout menu.

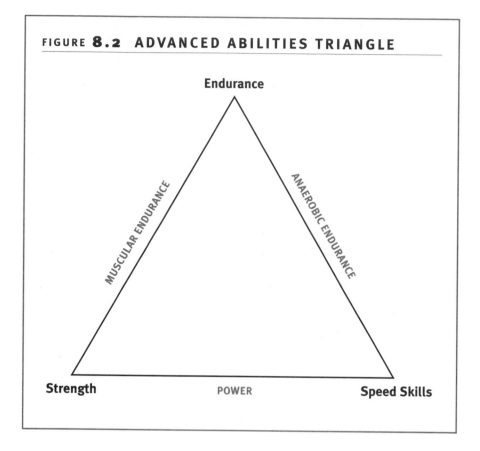

FIGURE **8.2** ADVANCED ABILITIES TRIANGLE

Anaerobic Endurance

Anaerobic endurance is a combination of speed skills and endurance. It is the ability to resist fatigue at high speeds and power outputs. It is only of importance for sprint-distance triathlons or when going head to head with a competitor toward the finish line. Half- and full-ironman-distance athletes do not need to develop their anaerobic endurance. There is growing evidence that anaerobic endurance type work may actually be detrimental to the aerobic endurance performance essential for these long-distance triathletes. See A workouts in the workout menu in Chapter 12.

Power

Power is the combination of speed skills and strength. It is used when you need to apply maximum force to the pedals very quickly, such as in sprinting. Power is important for off-road triathletes, who need to get up

TABLE 8.1 ABILITIES REQUIRED FOR TRIATHLON RACING

RACE DISTANCE	ENDURANCE	STRENGTH	SPEED	MUSCULAR ENDURANCE	ANAEROBIC ENDURANCE	POWER
Sprint	X	X	X	X	X	X
Olympic	X	X	X	X	X	
Xterra	X	X	X	X	X	X
Half-Ironman	X	X	X	X		
Ironman	X	X	X			

short, steep hills and power over obstacles. Power is important for the sprint-distance triathlete when speeding over short hills. Most road triathlon courses do not demand a great amount of power.

Elite ironman athletes need to train muscular endurance in order to maintain a high speed throughout the race. For all distances, the slower the athlete, the less valuable power and anaerobic endurance become and the more important it is to focus on the foundation abilities—endurance, strength, and speed skills. See Table 8.1 for more information on abilities required for triathlons.

ANALYZE YOUR PERSONAL ABILITIES

Use the personal strengths and weaknesses calculator in Table 8.2 to determine where your personal abilities lie. Rate the statements in Table 8.2 in the order in which they describe you best. Score foundation abilities one to three—one for the athlete statement that describes you best and three for the statement that describes you least. Score the advanced abilities four to six, with four describing you best and six describing you least.

CALCULATE YOUR LIMITERS

A limiter is a race-specific weakness. To calculate your limiters you must consider how your personal abilities match the demands of your

TABLE 8.2 CALCULATOR FOR PERSONAL STRENGTHS AND WEAKNESSES

ATHLETE STATEMENTS	FOUNDATION ABILITIES	SCORE (1 TO 3)
Just finishing the bike leg of a race is difficult for me.	Endurance	
I am passed by lots of other triathletes on hills.	Strength	
I am a "masher." I push big gears slowly.	Speed skills	

ATHLETE STATEMENTS	ADVANCED ABILITIES	SCORE (4 TO 6)
Even on flat courses, my bike speed decreases near the end.	Muscular endurance	
As the bike portion of a race gets shorter, I do worse relative to those in my category.	Anaerobic endurance	
In short races I struggle to get over short "power" hills.	Power	

event. You may have marvelous anaerobic endurance, but if your goal is to race in an ironman, that ability will not be particularly useful for you. Conversely, your anaerobic endurance may be weak, but as an ironman athlete you don't need to worry about improving it. Spending time improving your anaerobic endurance will not enhance your performance in ironman-distance events. By focusing your training time on improving the ability that will bring you the most performance gains in your chosen event, you will train accurately and specifically.

Use the limiter calculator in Table 8.3 to figure out your limiter—what is holding you back from peak performance at your chosen race.

A STORY OF OVER-LIVING, UNDER-SLEEPING, GREED, AND GOAL DILUTION

Dave trained hard, had a dedicated coach, was on a good team, and was single with few responsibilities. He had everything in his favor. Dave was, however, on a performance plateau. He was terribly frustrated, getting the same results every season of racing while his friends steadily got faster. Dave followed his coach's training plans diligently, but he doggedly refused advice about his lifestyle. You see, Dave sometimes worked in excess of 100 hours a week and at times worked through the night. He would go home long enough to do his training ride and then he would head back to work.

This was a serious case of "over-living." The best training plan in the world will not bring you peak performance if you do not take care of your body. As an athlete in training, you need at least 8 hours of sleep per night to truly reach your athletic potential. If you are not sleeping that much, you are holding yourself back.

Dave also liked to compete in every race in his home state and the neighboring three states. One weekend he planned to work until 6 p.m. on Friday, drive north to a different state, race there on Saturday, then, after the race, drive two states over and race there on Sunday. (Fortunately his coach managed to derail that plan and limit him to racing only on Sunday.) Dave was greedy for race results, but he had diluted his goals so much that he could not achieve any of them. He followed this pattern year after year and ultimately began to question whether his genetics were his limiting factor.

I am not coaching Dave anymore, and he never did listen to my advice about his lifestyle. If you are reading this, Dave, here is the biggest challenge of your racing career: Get 8 hours of sleep a night!

Steps to Calculate Your Limiters

1. Use Table 8.3 to list the event demands in order of priority from 1 to 6. The most dominant event demand receives a score of 1.

2. Next, fill in your personal abilities scores calculated in Table 8.2, the personal strengths and weaknesses calculator. Your weakest foundation ability (endurance, force, or speed skills) scores 1 and your strongest foundation ability scores 3. Your weakest advanced ability (muscular endurance, anaerobic endurance, or power) scores 4 and your strongest advanced ability scores 6.

3. Add up the scores for each ability from both lists to find your limiter. An ability that is not listed as an event demand does not receive a score.

4. The ability that has the lowest total score is your limiter.

For example (see Table 8.4):

Goal: Finish under 6 hours at the St. Croix Half Ironman® Triathlon. St. Croix is a hilly race in a hot, humid climate and is sometimes windy.

As shown in Table 8.4, for this athlete, endurance is the primary limiter. This athlete should focus the bulk of his or her training time on endurance. Speed skills and force have close scores and will both be part of the training plan. Muscular endurance will be a low priority. Anaerobic endurance and power do not receive a score as they are not event demands for the St. Croix Half Ironman®. Anaerobic endurance and power will not be specifically trained at all.

TABLE **8.3** LIMITER CALCULATOR

EVENT DEMANDS	SCORE
Endurance	
Force	
Speed skills	
Muscular endurance	
Anaerobic endurance	
Power	

PERSONAL ABILITIES	SCORE
Endurance	
Force	
Speed skills	
Muscular endurance	
Anaerobic endurance	
Power	

LIMITERS	SCORE
Endurance	
Force	
Speed skills	
Muscular endurance	
Anaerobic endurance	
Power	

TABLE **8.4** LIMITER CALCULATOR EXAMPLE FOR THE ST. CROIX HALF IRONMAN®

EVENT DEMANDS	SCORE
Endurance	1
Force	2
Speed skills	3
Muscular endurance	4

WEAKNESSES TO STRENGTHS	SCORE
Speed skills	1
Endurance	2
Force	3
Anaerobic endurance	4
Power	5
Muscular endurance	6

LIMITERS	SCORE
Endurance	3
Speed skills	4
Force	5
Muscular endurance	10

Other Limiters

There are other factors to consider that may be keeping you from peak performance. These factors may be even more important than any of the physical training abilities analyzed above. Read through the following list and see if you can identify something that is holding you back. If you do identify an area to improve and you improve it, congratulations! You have just raised the ceiling of your athletic potential.

- Insufficient sleep
- Mediocre nutrition
- Excess stress
- Frequent injury and illness (probably due to the above three)
- Goal dilution (the more goals, the lower the likelihood each will be achieved)
- Lack of race experience
- Inattention to proper recovery techniques
- Poor body composition
- Repeating tactical mistakes (poor pacing, lack of warm-up, disqualification, eating the wrong prerace meal, missing your start)
- Lack of family and financial support
- Insufficient time available to train

9 Periodize Your Training Plan

Periodization is a process of structuring training into separate phases, cycles, or periods. Each period builds on the previous one to ensure gradual progression of your fitness and timing of performance peaks with "A" events. Athletes who train in a random and aimless manner will have random and aimless and fitness peaks. This is fine for athletes who just want to stay in shape, but not for those focused on a specific event. Athletes focused on specific events need to time their peak fitness with their goal event. A well-structured plan will help you reach your goals in a timely manner. Periodization is a planning process that organizes training to guarantee success.

An annual training plan outlines your whole season, giving you guidance through the days and weeks of training leading up to your goal event. The first step in designing a periodized training plan is to construct your annual training plan.

DESIGNING YOUR ANNUAL TRAINING PLAN

To get started, you need a large calendar with a box for every day of the year, a red pen, and a pencil. See Appendix A for a blank calendar.

Goals

At the top of the calendar in red pen write up to three goals you want to achieve this season. See Chapter 8 for goal-setting guidelines. Always keep your goals visible and next to your training plan. Also write your goals in red pen on the date when each of them will be completed.

Races

Each race you do this season should be prioritized as A, B, or C. A events are usually the same as your goals. The number of A events you can realistically peak for depends upon the distance of the event and the length of recovery required after the event. Generally, it is best to limit yourself to three or less A events per season. If your goal event is an ironman-distance race or longer, it is recommended that you only do one or two of races of this distance per season, as they demand lengthy recovery periods. Scheduling more than three A events dilutes your goals and reduces the likelihood you will be in peak condition for any of them. Your periodization schedule will be organized around these A events. You will build your race-specific fitness as they approach and then rest and taper to bring your body into peak fitness.

B events are important races at which you want to do well. You will arrive at B races rested but not at your peak, and you will not take the time to do a full taper for a B race. The number of B races that you schedule should depend on the length of each race and the time it takes for your body to recover afterward.

C events are the least important events for you. C events will be part of your training schedule and will take the place of a workout that week. There is no recommended limit to the number of C races you do each season; it is highly personal. If one of your limiters is lack of race experience, or if you really enjoy being part of a race, it will be valuable for you to do lots of C races. If you are an experienced racer, or if you find racing to be stressful, too many C races may detract from your training and you are better off doing just a few. C races are training races. You should not be concerned about the outcome of your placing in a C race. Be careful not to squander peak fitness on C races and arrive at your goal event past your peak.

A races

Write your A-priority races on your calendar in red pen.

Now you have the basic framework of your annual training plan. You have your goals and A-priority events (these are usually the same) marked in red pen. These are the parts of your season that will not change. You should use pencil for the rest of your annual training plan. An annual traning plan is an evolving document and should be consulted and updated regularly.

TRAINING PERIODS

An annual training plan is made up of nine training periods. Each training period develops a specific facet of your fitness, eventually bringing you into peak shape at your goal event. See Table 9.1 for an explanation of each period.

Preparation Period

The Prep period can last three to four weeks. This is the phase when you gradually ease back into a training routine. Strength training starts in the gym with very light weights and high repetitions. The focus of strength training is to strengthen your joints and connective tissues before you make big gains in muscle strength. This is the period to slowly build up the endurance your body needs to start the "real" training.

Base Periods

The Base period can last 12 to 16 weeks. The Base period is divided into Base 1, Base 2 and Base 3. Each period lasts three to four weeks. During the Base training you develop the foundation, or "base" fitness, needed to be a well-conditioned athlete. The Base period of training focuses on the foundation abilities of endurance, skills, and force (strength)—the core of your peak performance. If you skimp on this period of your training, your peak performance will be inconsistent and unpredictable.

Base 1

The primary focus of Base 1 is aerobic endurance, skills, and strength. Aerobic endurance is built with long, easy workouts from the E1 and E2 series of workouts in the workout menu at the back of the book. These E1 and E2 workouts can be rides, or you can cross train with another aerobic activity such as cross-country skiing. Skills are built with drills on the bike, such as any of the S series workouts in the workout menu. Force is built in the gym by lifting weights.

Base 2

At this point, cross training should be reduced and most workouts should be done on the bike. The focus should still be on developing aerobic endurance (E1 and E2 workouts), skills (S workouts), and force. To transfer strength you have developed in the gym to the bike, introduce hills to your rides with E3 and F1 workouts. If one of your personal ability limiters is a foundation ability, emphasize it in your training during this period. Short-course athletes introduce muscular-endurance training with tempo training and cruise intervals (M1 workouts). Long-course athletes remain focused on the foundation abilities (E, F, S).

Base 3

In Base 3, cross training should end and all workouts should be done on the bike. Emphasis should be placed on your personal ability limiter if it is a foundation ability. Aerobic endurance and skills are still trained. You should be tapering out of the gym and building your force-production ability on the bike with the introduction of longer and steeper hills (F2 and F3 workouts).

Build Periods

You can have up to eight weeks of Build-period training before your first Peak of the season. There are two Build periods, each three to four weeks in duration. During the Build periods, your focus changes from training your limiters to training your strengths—what you are good at and what wins you races. The Build period is for race-specific preparation.

Build 1

Workouts should become increasingly race-specific. Analyze the demands of your goal event in detail. Your training should imitate the distance, course, and conditions you will encounter in your race. A higher proportion of the workouts should be combo swim-to-bike or bike-to-run workouts. When training for ironman-distance events, your Base and Build periods will look similar. Short-course athletes will need to place more emphasis on training the advanced abilities—muscular endurance, anaerobic endurance, and power.

TABLE **9.1** PERIODIZATION SUMMARY

PERIOD	DURATION	TRAINING FOCUS
Preparation	3–4 weeks	Gradual return to training. Start strength training. Focus on endurance and skill building.
Base 1	3–4 weeks	Establish aerobic endurance, build sport-specific skills, and build strength with weight training.
Base 2	3–4 weeks	Continue to build aerobic endurance, sport-specific skills, and strength. Add some rolling hills to build force. Introduce muscular endurance training with cruise intervals. Spend time training your personal ability limiter.
Base 3	3–4 weeks	Continue to build aerobic endurance, sport-specific skills, and strength. Add some longer hills to build force and muscular endurance. Focus training on your personal ability limiter.
Build 1	3–4 weeks	Focus training on goal-event demands and your personal strengths. Maintain endurance, skills, and force. Continue training your personal ability limiter.
Build 2	3–4 weeks	Focus training on goal-event demands.
Peak	1–2 weeks	Reduce total training volume; maintain workout frequency and intensity.
Race	1 week	Reduce total training volume; maintain workout frequency and intensity. Perfect pre-race tactics and strategy.
Mid-Season Transition	1–2 weeks	May be total rest or cross training with low-intensity activity. Mentally refresh.
Post-Season Transition	2–8 weeks	Stay active with unstructured workouts and cross training. Rest and recover.

Build 2

Workouts should be very race-specific and geared toward your strengths. Continue with combo workouts at race speed and/or at race distance. Practice transitions. Rehearse all race logistics including transitions, pre-race meal, equipment selection, race warm-up, and race nutrition and hydration strategies.

Peak Period

The Peak period can last one to two weeks. During the Peak period you unload the fatigue you have accumulated during the Build period. It is best to keep the frequency of your workouts the same, shorten their duration, and decrease the total amount of time at higher intensities. Keep short race speed repeats in the schedule, such as 4 x 90-second taper repeats.

Race Period

The Race period lasts one week and starts seven days before your goal event. For a Sunday race, the race period starts the previous Monday. This is the week when you make your final race preparations and focus on your pre-race strategies and tactics. Workouts during this week should be easy and short, containing short, race-pace efforts that are long enough to keep your body used to moving at race pace but not long enough to cause any fatigue. During this week your total activity level will be lower, and you must reduce your calorie intake to avoid packing on a few extra pounds before race day.

Transition Periods
Post-season transition

This transition phase starts immediately after your final race of the season. It may last from four to eight weeks. During this time you should not follow a structured training plan. It is a good idea to ditch your heart rate monitor and power meter and just train by feel. Stay active but do whatever inspires you for that day's workout, and keep the intensity of your workouts low. If you developed overuse injuries during the race season, now is the time to take an extended break and let them fully heal. Cross training is perfect for this time of year. Try cross-country skiing, rollerblading, backpacking, or anything that is fresh and new. Now is the time to paint your house, sand your deck, and tend to your family (not necessarily in that order).

Mid-season transition

If your season is structured with two peaks, it is a good idea to take a mid-season transition period. This can last from one to two weeks. This midseason transition is an important refresher week to allow your body to recover from a peak performance and from the training leading up to that performance.

Establish Duration of Training Periods

Preparation, Base, and Build periods last for three to four weeks each. The final week of each training period is a rest week. On three-week periods, you train for two weeks then rest the third. Four-week periods have you training for three weeks and resting in week four. As a general rule, beginners and older athletes should follow a three-week training period. If recovery from workouts is a limiter for you, also use a three-week period. Otherwise, four-week periods work well. Combinations of periods lengths can be put together to suit your needs. Some athletes can handle large volumes of low-intensity training without a rest. These athletes can follow a four week period during Base training. However, these same athletes may not recover quickly from high-intensity work and need to follow three-week periods during Build training.

Schedule Your Training Periods

To schedule your training periods, start at your A priority event and work backward. Label the week of your A-priority event Race week. Label the next two weeks up on the calendar as Peak weeks. Next, fill in your Build 2, Build 1, Base 3, Base 2, Base 1, and Prep periods. Label the last week in each of the Prep, Base 1, Base 2, Base 3, Build 1, and Build 2 as a rest week.

Set Your Objectives

All training periods need training objectives. Training objectives are mini goals and milestones that you complete during a training period. Give yourself a maximum of five objectives per period, write these objectives on your calendar at the beginning of each period, and tick them off as you accomplish them. A series of objectives will keep your training headed in the right direction and your performance timing on track. Completing a series of objectives leads you directly to

your goal and can be valuable in building self-confidence—a key ingre-
dient for success. It is very satisfying to look back over your training
plan and see that you have accomplished all of your objectives.

There are two types of objectives: turnstile objectives and performance objectives. Turnstile objectives are those that you simply complete by a certain date. Turnstile objectives are the best types of
objectives to set for yourself if you are a novice triathlete in your first
season of racing. "Run 3 miles by March 31" or "ride four times a week"
are turnstile objectives. "Run 10 miles in less than one hour by May
31," however, is a performance objective. You have a certain performance level to achieve in order to successfully complete this objective.
Performance objectives are appropriate for seasoned athletes seeking
maximum performance gains. A combination of performance and
turnstile objectives works the best for most athletes.

To design your objectives, you must consider the focus of the training period, your goals, your limiters, and the training principles set out
in Chapter 6. Limit yourself to five (or less) objectives per training
period. Decide which ability the objective addresses and then design
an objective that will challenge that ability.

SAMPLE TRAINING OBJECTIVES FOR BASE 1 PERIOD

1. **Training consistency:** Strength train three times per week.

2. **Muscular strength:** Increase squat weight by 10 percent.

3. **Endurance:** Do a ride of two hours or more each week.

4. **Endurance:** Complete Lake Loop road ride with a PE of 5 in less than an hour.

5. **Fun:** Reserve every Saturday afternoon for family time.

CHAPTER

10 Create Your Personal Training Plan

In Chapter 8 you identified your strengths and weaknesses, the demands of your goal event, and your limiters. In Chapter 9 you created your annual training plan with training periods, training focus, and training objectives. In this chapter you will fill in the details to create your daily and weekly training plan.

Plan your daily workouts using the following:

- The training principles set out in Chapter 6: overload, adaptation, load progression, specificity, individuality, and reversibility.
- The training guidelines for each training period set out in Chapter 9.
- The objectives you established for each training period in Chapter 9.

SET YOUR TOTAL ANNUAL TRAINING HOURS

To decide how many hours to train each week, you must consider the training principles: overload, adaptation, and load progression. You need to schedule a volume of training that combines overload with enough rest, allowing you to adapt and grow stronger. As you adapt to a certain level of overload, you must progressively increase it (training principle number three is load progression) to reach greater levels of fitness.

The total number of hours you trained last season is a benchmark value you will use to decide the number of hours you need to train this season. Your total annual hours trained include time spent swimming, biking, running, strength training, and cross training. If your previous season was a success—with no prolonged illness, overtraining, or overuse injuries—take the annual hours you trained and add up to 10-percent more. If you had a season plagued with injuries, illness, or overtraining, you need to reduce the number of annual hours you trained by 10 percent or more. Review your training logs from prior years to calculate these numbers. More hours are not always better.

If you are a newbie triathlete in your first or second year of training, you cannot base your training hours on the prior year and you need to do a little guesswork. Assign yourself the number of training hours in Preparation period week one that you consider to be very comfortable and not challenging, then read down that column in Table 10.1. Be conservative in allocating your training hours. It is far better to be undertrained, healthy, and happy than overtrained, sick, and injured.

CALCULATE YOUR TOTAL WEEKLY TRAINING HOURS

Once you have calculated your total number of annual training hours, go to Table 10.1 to determine the number of hours to train each week.

Your weekly training volume in the Prep period will be the lowest of the season. Volume will increase gradually during the Base training period as you progressively develop endurance. In the Build period, the weekly volume is reduced and the intensity becomes more race specific. There is a limit to the training load to which your body can adapt.

As you increase the intensity of your training, you must decrease the volume. In a nutshell, you build your aerobic endurance early in the season with long rides, then you build your race-specific fitness later with race-like rides.

Set Your Bike-Training Hours

In triathlons, more than half of the total race time is usually spent on the bike leg. As a general rule, half of your total training time can be assigned to bike training. Athletes who are already excellent cyclists are exceptions to this rule, and they may benefit by placing an emphasis on their weaker sports.

SCHEDULE YOUR DAILY WORKOUTS

What exactly will you do each day when you jump on your bike?

Preparation Period

PREP PERIOD SAMPLE WEEK

MON.	TUES.	WED.	THURS.	FRI.	SAT.	SUN.
	1:00 S1b		1:00 S1a	1:00 E1e optional		2:00 E1e

The Prep period is a key time to look at your cycling equipment. Your weekly bike-training volume is at the lowest point of the year and the intensity is very low, so it is a perfect time to adapt to a new bike or any position changes you need to make to your current bike. If you have not considered it before, schedule a professional bike fit session during the Preparation period. This will ensure that all of your training for the new season is done in your optimal position.

All key bike workouts during the Prep period should focus on skills and endurance. Schedule three to four bike rides per week consisting of at least one endurance ride, two skills rides, and an additional endurance ride if you have time. Choose from S1a, S1b, S1c, S1d, S1e, S1f, and S3c on the workout menu (see Chapter 12) for skills rides, and select from any of the E1 workouts for endurance rides. Assign 40 percent of your weekly hours to the first endurance ride and 20 percent

TABLE **10.1**　WEEKLY TRAINING HOURS

Period	week	ANNUAL HOURS								
		200	250	300	350	400	450	500	550	600
Prep	all	3.5	4.0	5.0	6.0	7.0	7.5	8.5	9.0	10.0
Base I	1	4.0	5.0	6.0	7.0	8.0	9.0	10.0	11.0	12.0
	2	5.0	6.0	7.0	8.5	9.5	10.5	12.0	13.0	14.5
	3	5.5	6.5	8.0	9.5	10.5	12.0	13.5	14.5	16.0
	4	3.0	3.5	4.0	5.0	5.5	6.5	7.0	8.0	8.5
Base II	1	4.0	5.5	6.5	7.5	8.5	9.5	10.5	12.5	12.5
	2	5.0	6.5	7.5	9.0	10.0	11.5	12.5	14.0	15.0
	3	5.5	7.0	8.5	10.0	11.0	12.5	14.0	15.5	17.0
	4	3.0	3.5	4.5	5.0	5.5	6.5	7.0	8.0	8.5
Base III	1	4.5	5.5	7.0	8.0	9.0	10.0	11.0	12.5	13.5
	2	5.0	6.5	8.0	9.5	10.5	12.0	13.5	14.5	16.0
	3	6.0	7.5	9.0	10.5	11.5	13.0	15.0	16.5	18.0
	4	3.0	3.5	4.5	5.0	5.5	6.5	7.0	8.0	8.5
Build I	1	5.0	6.5	8.0	9.0	10.0	11.5	12.5	14.0	15.5
	2	5.0	6.5	8.0	9.0	10.0	11.5	12.5	14.0	15.5
	3	5.0	6.5	8.0	9.0	10.0	11.5	12.5	14.0	15.5
	4	3.0	3.5	4.5	5.0	5.5	6.5	7.0	8.0	8.5
Build II	1	5.0	6.0	7.0	8.5	9.5	10.5	12.0	13.0	14.5
	2	5.0	6.0	7.0	8.5	9.5	10.5	12.0	13.0	14.5
	3	5.0	6.0	7.0	8.5	9.5	10.5	12.0	13.0	14.5
	4	3.0	3.5	4.5	5.0	5.5	6.5	7.0	8.0	8.5
Peak	1	4.0	5.5	6.5	7.5	8.5	9.5	10.5	11.5	13.0
	2	3.5	4.0	5.0	6.0	6.5	7.5	8.5	9.5	10.0
Race	all	3.0	3.5	4.5	5.0	5.5	6.5	7.0	8.0	8.5
Trans.	all	3.0	3.5	4.5	5.0	5.5	6.5	7.0	8.0	8.5

650	700	750	800	850	900	950	1000	1050	1100	1150	1200
11.0	12.0	12.5	13.5	14.5	15.0	16.0	17.0	17.5	18.5	19.5	20.0
12.5	14.0	14.5	15.5	16.5	17.5	18.5	19.5	20.5	21.5	22.5	23.5
15.5	16.5	18.0	19.0	20.0	21.5	22.5	24.0	25.0	26.0	27.5	28.5
17.5	18.5	20.0	21.5	22.5	24.0	25.5	26.5	28.0	29.5	30.5	32.0
9.0	10.0	10.5	11.5	12.0	12.5	13.5	14.0	14.5	15.5	16.0	17.0
13.0	14.5	16.0	17.0	18.0	19.0	20.0	21.0	22.0	23.0	24.0	25.0
16.5	17.5	19.0	20.0	21.5	22.5	24.0	25.0	26.5	27.5	29.0	30.0
18.0	19.5	21.0	22.5	24.0	25.0	26.5	28.0	29.5	31.0	32.0	33.5
9.0	10.0	10.5	11.5	12.0	12.5	13.5	14.0	15.0	15.5	16.0	17.0
14.5	15.5	17.0	18.0	19.0	20.0	21.0	22.5	23.5	25.0	25.5	27.0
17.0	18.5	20.0	21.5	23.0	24.0	25.0	26.5	28.0	29.5	30.5	32.0
19.0	20.5	22.0	23.5	25.0	26.5	28.0	29.5	31.0	32.5	33.5	35.0
9.0	10.0	10.5	11.5	12.0	12.5	13.5	14.0	15.0	15.5	16.0	17.0
16.0	17.5	19.0	20.5	21.5	22.5	24.0	25.0	26.5	28.0	29.0	30.0
16.0	17.5	19.0	20.5	21.5	22.5	24.0	25.0	26.5	28.0	29.0	30.0
16.0	17.5	19.0	20.5	21.5	22.5	24.0	25.0	26.5	28.0	29.0	30.0
9.0	10.0	10.5	11.5	12.0	12.5	13.5	14.0	15.0	15.5	16.0	17.0
15.5	16.5	18.0	19.0	20.5	21.5	22.5	24.0	25.0	26.5	27.0	28.5
15.5	16.5	18.0	19.0	20.5	21.5	22.5	24.0	25.0	26.5	27.0	28.5
15.5	16.5	18.0	19.0	20.5	21.5	22.5	24.0	25.0	26.5	27.0	28.5
9.0	10.0	10.5	11.5	12.0	12.5	13.5	14.0	15.0	15.5	16.0	17.0
13.5	14.5	16.0	17.0	18.0	19.0	20.0	21.0	22.0	23.5	24.0	25.0
11.0	11.5	12.5	13.5	14.5	15.0	16.0	17.0	17.5	18.5	19.0	20.0
9.0	10.0	10.5	11.5	12.0	12.5	13.5	14.0	15.0	15.5	16.0	17.0
9.0	10.0	10.5	11.5	12.0	12.5	13.5	14.0	15.0	15.5	16.0	17.0

of your weekly hours to each of the other rides. Spread these rides out throughout the week.

Cross training with a rhythmic aerobic activity such as cross-country skiing or rollerblading can be substituted for any of the endurance rides, but be sure to do two skills rides on the bike each week. Most of these skills rides can be done on rollers or an indoor trainer.

Base 1

BASE 1 SAMPLE WEEK						
MON.	TUES.	WED.	THURS.	FRI.	SAT.	SUN.
	1:00 S1b		1:00 S1a	1:00 E1e or limiter		3:00 E2b

Continue focusing on endurance and skills. Ride three to four times per week, including at least two skills rides (S) and one endurance ride (E2b). Add an additional endurance ride (any E1 ride) if you have time. Increase the duration of the primary endurance ride by a little each week, but maintain the duration of all the other rides. In Base 1 you may still cross train in place of the endurance ride. Add a few small, rolling hills to your endurance sessions. Keep the two skills rides on the bike each week—on rollers, an indoor trainer, or outdoors.

Base 2

BASE 2 SAMPLE WEEK						
MON.	TUES.	WED.	THURS.	FRI.	SAT.	SUN.
	1:00 M1a or M1b		1:00 F1a or limiter	1:00 S1b		3:15 E2f

Reduce cross training and increase weekly time on the bike. Ride three to five times per week. During Base 2 include one skills ride (S), one endurance ride (E2f), and a ride with longer hills (F1a, F1c). Your fourth ride of the week should address your limiter. If you add a fifth ride, choose from any E1 ride.

Short-course athletes should begin some tempo rides to establish their muscular endurance ability. Choose ride M1a for this. Combo workouts—swim-to-bike and bike-to-run—are essential for triathletes and should be included in Base 2. While this book focuses on bike training only, any of the bike sessions in this plan can be linked with a swim or run to form a combo workout.

Base 3

MON.	TUES.	WED.	THURS.	FRI.	SAT.	SUN.
	1:15 M1d or M1e		1:15 F1a or limiter	1:00 S1b		3:30 E3b or E3c

BASE 3 SAMPLE WEEK

Cross training should be eliminated in Base 3. Ride three to five times per week, increasing the duration of endurance rides. Short-course athletes will do their longest rides of the season in Base 3. Long-course athletes will continue to extend their ride duration in the Build periods. Include one endurance ride (E2f), one hilly ride (F1a or F1c), one skills ride (any S ride), and one limiter ride per week. Short-course athletes should continue to build muscular endurance—choose ride M1b.

Build Periods

BUILD 1 SAMPLE WEEK: LONG COURSE

MON.	TUES.	WED.	THURS.	FRI.	SAT.	SUN.
	1:30 F1c		1:00 S1b	1:15 strongest ability		5:00 E4a

BUILD 1 SAMPLE WEEK: SHORT COURSE

MON.	TUES.	WED.	THURS.	FRI.	SAT.	SUN.
	1:15 A2aL		1:30 M4a	1:30 strongest ability		3:15 E3c

This is when your specific race preparation should be done. Short-course athletes should focus on higher, race-like intensities, develop advanced abilities (muscular endurance, anaerobic endurance, and power), and practice speedy transitions. Long-course athletes will continue to focus on the foundation abilities (endurance, force, and skills) and on perfecting the fueling regime and pacing strategies they will use on race day.

The Build period is the time to focus on your strengths. Include one ride per week to build your strongest ability. Examine your goal race carefully to decide exactly what type of training you should do in the Build period. Mimic the type of course, duration of the race, terrain, and environmental conditions as closely as possible during endurance rides.

During the Build period, short-course triathletes should do some practice races as tune ups for their peak races. Long-course athletes should do some "dress rehearsal" workouts, mimicking the course and time of day and testing their equipment and nutrition strategy to be sure everything is working perfectly. Long-course athletes must finalize their race nutrition strategy during the Build periods.

Peak Period

Continue to ride three to five times per week during this period. Short-course triathletes should have one high-intensity bike workout per week in Peak 1 and Peak 2. This can be in the form of anaerobic endurance intervals, a hard group ride, or a B race. Long-course athletes should continue to do most of their riding at ironman-specific pace but reduce the duration of each ride. Total riding time should be less in Peak 2 than Peak 1. (Peak 1 is similar to Build 2 but with reduced volume.) Both short- and long-course athletes should do the final testing of their race equipment.

Race Period

Ride two to three times in addition to racing this week. Early in the week, do a one-hour skills ride, such as S1b. Midweek add a ride of one hour or less with four 90-second, race-intensity repeats, such as A5c. Two days prior to race day should be a rest day. The day before the race you should do a short, easy spin of 30 to 60 minutes, with one to four efforts of up to 90 seconds in duration at race intensity.

Transition Period

The only training rules to abide by during the transition period are to keep it easy and keep it fun. Allow your body to recover from hard training and intense racing.

TRAINING JOURNAL

Once you are following the training plan you created, it is essential to keep a training journal to log exactly what you do and keep track of your progress. Training journal information is most useful to look back on in order to identify trends, causes of mishaps and successes. The more detailed records you can keep of your training hours and performance benchmarks (tests, key training sessions, and races) the closer you can dial in on the perfect plan. A training journal can boost your confidence prior to an "A" race when you review all the objectives you have accomplished and training sessions completed leading up to the event. You can photocopy the blank training journal in Appendix B to use or create your own. The best online training journal tool is free and can be found at www.trainingbible.com. This provides a basic journal to track your training. For an additional subscription fee you can upgrade to a training journal with the ability to save heart rate and power files, graph various data points, and summarize information over time. Tasks such as calculating the total the number of hours you trained last year are done with a single click of the mouse.

Daily Information Gathering

Fill your training journal out every day while the information is fresh in your mind.

Daily metrics

Sleep, fatigue, stress, soreness, resting heart rate, and weight are daily metrics which indicate your general health status. These will tell you if you are recovering sufficiently from your workouts, and keep you aware of the big picture of how you are doing. An upswing in any of these indicators is a warning sign something is going on that needs your attention. Score sleep, fatigue, stress, and soreness on a 1–7 scale with 1 being best and 7 being worst. Take your resting heart rate shortly after waking while you are still in bed as this is the most consistent time of day. An overnight resting heart rate jump of five beats per minute is often a warning you are about to get sick. Backing off from a hard training session on this day would be prudent. A low resting heart rate usually means you are rested and ready to work hard.

Also record your daily body weight in your journal first thing in the morning. Large weight fluctuations are red flags.

Workout Information

In Appendix B, the blank training journal S, B, R, and O stand for swim, bike, run and other. Circle the appropriate letter and note the duration, weather, route, distance, and time of the workout. Also log the time you spendt in each training zone by the appropriate number. Under workout rating, record how the workout felt. Was it easy, moderate, or hard? Short or long? Did it feel like a death march or go by effortlessly? Comparing number data such as distance, time, and heart rate with this subjective information provides clues to any training plan modifications you need to make. If you thought a 30-minute heart rate zone one spin felt like an arduous death ride, you should put a lot more recovery time in your plan.

Notes

Write anything that comes to mind here. Sometimes the seemingly most irrelevant comments are tell-tales when viewed with the benefit of hindsight.

Race

Record race splits, results, and any extra race notes here.

Weekly summary

Keep a running tally of training data in the weekly summary. The blank row is for cross training data.

CHAPTER

11

Pre-Built
Training Plans

This chapter contains sample training plans, using the principles outlined in this book, to help you in design your own custom plan. It is assumed that you will be swimming, running, strength training, core training, and doing flexibility work along with the bike training. For the sake of simplicity, the following plans include bike training only.

PLAN ONE: **24-WEEK IRONMAN-DISTANCE**

RACE DISTANCE: Swim 2.4 miles, bike 112 miles, run 26.2 miles

This plan is designed for a triathlete who can comfortably train a total of 10 hours per week swimming, cycling, and running at the start of the program. Half of the weekly training time will be spent cycling. The plan starts with one Preparation period week consisting of four to five hours cycling (five to six hours should be on swimming, running, core training, strength training, and flexibility). Every fourth week of the plan is a rest week. Weekly volume peaks with 10 hours of cycling in the second and third weeks of Build 2 (see Table 11.1).

Strongest Abilities and Limiters

Your limiter should be trained during Base 2 and 3. For ironman-distance training, it should be chosen from the foundation abilities: endurance, force, or skills. Your strongest ability is trained during Build 1 and Build 2. For ironman-distance training your strongest ability should also be chosen from the foundation abilities.

For example, in weeks six to 13, an athlete with a limiter of skills and whose strongest ability is force will do a ride on Friday addressing a skills limiter, such as S1aL. In weeks 14 to 19 the Friday ride will focus on this athlete's strongest ability, force, with a ride such as F1a.

Additional Plan Notes

Schedule your long runs midweek to allow adequate recovery before your long ride on the weekend. Add a short transition run of 15 minutes after any bike session. If your bike-to-run transition is weak, include a 15-minute transition run after most of your rides. See pages 158–159 for a detailed training plan.

PLAN TWO: **24-WEEK OFF-ROAD TRIATHLON**

RACE DISTANCE: Swim 1,500m, mountain bike 30km, run 10km

This plan is for the triathlete who has already accomplished the challenge of finishing an off-road triathlon and is looking to improve upon time and placing, as well as for off-road triathletes aiming to win. During the Base periods, the plan progressively increases endurance and addresses limiters. During the Build periods, intensity is increased, the strongest ability is trained, and endurance is maintained. Two Peak training weeks fine-tune fitness for the A race, and two B races are included in the schedule as training races (see Table 11.2).

This plan emphasizes off-road cycling skills. Both bike-handling and pedaling skills are primary event demands for off-road triathlons, and all off-road triathletes should work on these skills during every ride. (Skills and other abilities can be trained within the same ride.) Pedaling efficiently while relaxed on bumpy terrain is a key skill trained during workout S6aL, which is done often during this plan. S6aL is a low-intensity session and can be used as a skill-building ride and also as a recovery session. Any ride in this plan can be done off road to build skills. As a general rule, at least two rides per week should be off road—even more if you are not confident of your skills in the dirt. However, off-road riding is more stressful on your body than road riding, so athletes who are confident off road may choose to train on pavement more often.

Mountain Biking versus Road Riding:

The key difference between road riding and mountain biking is the more stochastic nature of power outputs produced off road. Generally, in road triathlons you accelerate up to cruising speed and then maintain it for the duration of your event. This is not the case when riding off road. Mountain biking involves a constant series of accelerating and decelerating through corners, over obstacles, and over hills. To be a good mountain biker, you need to pay attention to this variable nature of power production and ensure that you train specifically for it. Steady-state road riding, meaning riding with even power output, builds steady-state fitness, which is important for a non-drafting road triathlon. Mountain biking will adapt the body to perform optimally on off-road courses. See pages 160–61 for a detailed training plan.

PLAN THREE: **24-WEEK HALF-IRONMAN–DISTANCE**

RACE DISTANCE: Swim 1.2 miles, bike 56 miles, run 13.1 miles

This plan is designed to perfectly prepare an athlete for a half-ironman-distance triathlon. Every fourth week is a rest week. Base 1 trains the foundation abilities, endurance, and skills with the highest volume week totaling four hours and 30 minutes. Base 2 trains the cycling limiter and force in addition to endurance and skills. Base 3 starts training the advanced ability of muscular endurance with tempo intervals in addition to the limiter, force, and endurance. Skills training is integrated into every ride and does not have its own session in Base 3. The longest ride in Base 3 is three hours, and the highest volume week is seven hours. Build 1 continues training muscular endurance, force, and endurance. Limiter training is dropped in favor of training the strongest ability. Build 2 continues training the same abilities as Build 1 but focuses on volume. The longest ride is four hours and the highest volume week is eight hours and 45 minutes. Total volume drops during Peak 1 and Peak 2, but intensity is maintained. See pages 162–63 for a detailed training plan.

PLAN FOUR: **12-WEEK SPRINT-DISTANCE**

RACE DISTANCE: Swim 500 yards, bike 14 miles, run 5km

This plan is designed for active people who have never done a triathlon before. The goal of the athlete following this plan is simply to complete the distance and finish with a smile. Beginner triathletes should only train foundation abilities of endurance, force, and skills. The limiter is endurance—the primary event demand for any beginner athlete.

The first two periods on the training plan, Base 1 and Base 2, are three-week periods with two weeks of training and one week of rest. As the athlete becomes stronger, Base 3 is lengthened to three weeks of training and one week of rest. One Peak week and a final Race week complete the plan. See pages 164–65 for a detailed training plan.

TABLE 11.1 24-WEEK IRONMAN-DISTANCE PLAN

TRAINING WEEK	PERIOD	WEEK	MON.	TUES.	WED.	
1	Prep			1:00 S1a or S1b		
2	Base 1	1		1:00 S1a or S1b		
3	Base 1	2		1:00 S1a or S1b		
4	Base 1	3		1:15 S1a or S1b		
5	Base 1	4		1:00 S1a or S1b		
6	Base 2	1		1:00 F1a or F1c		
7	Base 2	2		1:15 F1a or F1c		
8	Base 2	3		1:15 F1a or F1c		
9	Base 2	4		1:00 E1e		
10	Base 3	1		1:15 F1a or F1c		
11	Base 3	2		1:30 F1a or F1c		
12	Base 3	3		1:30 F1a or F1c		
13	Base 3	4		1:00 E1e		
14	Build 1	1		1:15 F1a or F1c		
15	Build 1	2		1:30 F1a or F1c		
16	Build 1	3		1:30 F1a or F1c		
17	Build 1	4		1:00 E1e		
18	Build 2	1		1:30 F1a or F1c		
19	Build 2	2		1:30 F1a or F1c		
20	Build 2	3		1:30 F1a or F1c		
21	Build 2	4		1:00 E1e		
22	Peak 1	1		1:00 F1a or F1c		
23	Peak 2	2		1:00 E1e		
24	Race	1		0:45 S1b		

	THURS.	FRI.	SAT.	SUN.
	1:00 S1a or S1b	1:00 Optional E1e		2:00 E1e
	1:00 S1a or S1b	1:00 Optional E1e		3:00 E2b
	1:00 S1a or S1b	1:00 Optional E1e		3:30 E2b
	1:00 S1a or S1b	1:00 Optional E1e		3:45 E2b
	1:00 S1a or S1b	1:00 Optional E1e		2:00 E1e
	1:00 S1a or S1b	1:00 limiter		3:30 E2f
	1:00 S1a or S1b	1:15 limiter		4:00 E2f
	1:00 S1a or S1b	1:15 limiter		4:15 E2f
	1:00 S1a or S1b	1:00 limiter		2:00 E1e
	1:00 S1a–S1e	1:15 limiter		4:00 E3b or E3c
	1:00 S1a–S1e	1:15 limiter		4:30 E3b or E3c
	1:00 S1a–S1e	1:30 limiter		4:45 E3b or E3c
	1:00 S1a–S1e	1:00 limiter		2:00 E1e
	1:00 S1a–S1e	1:15 strongest		4:30 E4aL or E4bL
	1:00 S1a–S1e	1:15 strongest		5:00 E4aL or E4bL
	1:00 S1a–S1e	1:30 strongest		5:30 E4aL or E4bL
	1:00 S1a–S1e	off		2:00 E1e
	1:00 S1a–S1e	1:15 strongest ability		5:45 E4aL or E4bL
	1:00 S1a–S1e	1:30 strongest ability		6:00 E4aL or E4bL
	1:00 S1a–S1e	1:30 strongest ability		6:00 E4aL or E4bL
	1:00 S1a–S1e	1:00 limiter		2:00 E1e
	1:00 S1a–S1e	1:00 strongest ability		4:00 E4aL or E4bL
	1:00 S1a–S1e	0:30 strongest ability		2:30 E1e
	0:45 A5c	off	0:30 E1e	**Race Day**

TABLE 11.2 24-WEEK OFF-ROAD TRIATHLON PLAN

TRAINING WEEK	PERIOD	WEEK	MON.	TUES.	WED.	
1	Prep			S7aL 1:00		
2	Base 1	1		S1a or S1b 1:15		
3	Base 1	2		S7aL 1:30		
4	Base 1	3		S1a or S1b 1:30		
5	Base 1	4		S7aL 1:00		
6	Base 2	1		F1a or F1c 1:15		
7	Base 2	2		F1a or F1c 1:30		
8	Base 2	3		F1a or F1c 1:30		
9	Base 2	4		S6aL 1:00		
10	Base 3	1		M1b 1:00		
11	Base 3	2		M1b 1:30		
12	Base 3	3		M1b 1:45		
13	Base 3	4		E1eL 1:00		
14	Build 1	1		A2aL 1:15		
15	Build 1	2		A2aL 1:15		
16	Build 1	3		A2aL 1:15		
17	Build 1	4		S1a or S1b 1:00		
18	Build 2	1		A2b 1:15		
19	Build 2	2		A2b 1:15		
20	Build 2	3		A2b 1:15		
21	Build 2	4		S1b 1:00		
22	Peak 1	1		A2b 1:15		
23	Peak 2	2		A2aL 1:00		
24	Race	1		S1b 1:00		

THURS.	FRI.	SAT.	SUN.
S6aL 1:00	Optional E1eL 1:00		E1e 2:00
S6aL 1:00	Optional E1eL 1:00		E2b 2:30
S6aL 1:00	Optional E1eL 1:15		E2b 2:45
S6aL 1:00	Optional E1eL 1:30		E2b 3:00
S6aL 1:00	off		E1eL 2:00
M1a 1:00	limiter 1:15		E2f 2:45
M1a 1:30	limiter 1:5		E2f 3:15
M1a 1:30	limiter 1:30		E2f 3:30
E1eL 1:00	off		E1eL 2:00
F1d 1:15	limiter 1:30		E3b or E3c 3:00
F1d 1:30	limiter 1:30		E3b or E3c 3:30
F1d 2:00	limiter 1:30		E3b or E3c 3:30
S6aL 1:00	off		E1eL 2:00
M4a 1:30	strongest ability 1:30		E3c 3:15
M4a 1:30	strongest ability 1:30		E3c 3:15
M4a 1:30	strongest ability 1:30		E3c 3:15
E1eL 1:00	off		B Race 2:00
M4bL 1:30	strongest ability 1:30		E4aL 2:45
M4bL 1:30	strongest ability 1:30		E4aL 2:45
M4bL 1:30	strongest ability 1:30		E4aL 2:45
E1eL 1:00	off	M5b 0:30	B Race 2:00
M4bL 1:15	strongest ability 1:30		E4cL 2:30
M4bL 1:00	strongest ability 1:30		E4cL 2:00
A5c 0:45	off	M5b 0:30	**Race Day**

TABLE 11.3 24-WEEK HALF-IRONMAN–DISTANCE PLAN

TRAINING WEEK	PERIOD	WEEK	MON.	TUES.	WED.	
1	Prep			E1e 0:45		
2	Base 1	1		E1e 1:00		
3	Base 1	2		E1e 1:00		
4	Base 1	3		E1e 1:00		
5	Base 1	4		E1a 1:00		
6	Base 2	1		F1a 1:00		
7	Base 2	2		F1a 1:15		
8	Base 2	3		F1a 1:15		
9	Base 2	4		E1a 0:30		
10	Base 3	1		M1a 1:15		
11	Base 3	2		M1a 1:30		
12	Base 3	3		M1b 1:30		
13	Base 3	4		E1e 1:00		
14	Build 1	1		M1b 1:30		
15	Build 1	2		M1f 1:30		
16	Build 1	3		M1f 1:45		
17	Build 1	4		E1e 1:00		
18	Build 2	1		M1f 1:45		
19	Build 2	2		M1g 2:00		
20	Build 2	3		M1g 2:15		
21	Build 2	4		E1e 1:00		
22	Peak 1	1		M1f 2:00		
23	Peak 2	2		M1b 1:15		
24	Race	1		S1b 0:45		

THURS.	FRI.	SAT.	SUN.
S1aL 0:30	E1e optional 0:30		E2b 1:15
S1b 0:30	E1e optional 0:30		E2b 1:30
S1aL 0:45	E1e optional 0:30		E2b 1:45
S1b 1:00	E1e optional 0:30		E2b 2:00
S1aL 0:30			E1e 1:00
S1e 1:00	limiter 0:45		E2f 2:00
S1b 1:00	limiter 1:00		E2f 2:15
S1e 1:00	limiter 1:00		E2f 2:30
S1b 0:45	off		E1e 1:15
F1a 1:30	limiter 1:00		E3b 2:30
F1a 1:30	limiter 1:00		E3b 2:45
F1a 1:30	limiter 1:00		E3b 3:00
S1e 0:45	off		E1e 1:30
F1c 1:45	strongest ability 1:00		E3b 3:00
F1c 1:45	strongest ability 1:00		E3b 3:15
F1c 1:30	strongest ability 1:00		E3b 3:30
S1b 0:45	off		E1e 1:30
F1c 1:30	strongest ability 1:00		E4aL 3:30
F1c 1:30	strongest ability 1:00		E4aL 3:45
F1c 1:30	strongest ability 1:00		E4aL 4:00
S1a–S1e 1:00	off		E1e 2:00
F1a 1:15	strongest ability 1:00		E4aL 2:30
E1e 1:00	strongest ability 1:00		E2f 2:00
A5c 0:45	off	M5b 0:30	**Race Day**

TABLE **11.4** 12-WEEK BEGINNER SPRINT-DISTANCE PLAN

TRAINING WEEK	PERIOD	WEEK	MON.	TUES.	WED.	
1	Base 1	1			S1aL 0:30	
2	Base 1	2			S1aL 0:30	
3	Base 1	3			S1aL0:30	
4	Base 2	1			S1b 0:45	
5	Base 2	2			S1aL 0:45	
6	Base 2	3			S1b 0:45	
7	Base 3	1			S1aL 0:45	
8	Base 3	2			S1b 0:45	
9	Base 3	3			S1aL 0:45	
10	Base 3	4			S1b 0:30	
11	Peak 1	1			S1aL 0:30	
12	Race	1			S1b 0:30	

THURS.	FRI.	SAT.	SUN.
	S1b 0:30		E1e 0:45
	S1b 0:30		E1e 1:00
	E1e 0:30		E1e 0:30
	E1e 0:45		E2b 1:15
	E1e 0:45		E2b 1:30
	E1e 0:30		E2b 0:30
	E2b 1:00		E2f 1:30
	E2b 1:00		E2f 1:45
	E2b 1:00		E2f 2:00
	E1a 0:30		E1a 0:45
	E2b 0:45		E2b 1:00
	E1a 0:30		**Race Day**

PART FOUR

The Workouts

12 Workout Menus

Most of these workouts and the corresponding codes can be found at www.trainingbible.com. E workouts build aerobic endurance, F workouts build strength, S workouts improve skills and technique, M workouts improve muscular endurance, A workouts build anaerobic endurance, and P workouts improve power generation. The following menu of workouts is provided to give you the tools you need to design a training program specifically for you.

ENDURANCE WORKOUTS

E1a   **Recovery ride.** Very easy recovery spin in heart rate Zone 1 or below on a flat course or indoor trainer. Small chainring only. Light on the pedals.

E1e   **Recovery ride.** Ride in heart rate Zones 1–2 on a flat course. Put out a low effort with a comfortably high cadence.

E1eL   **Easy ride.** Mellow, easy, relaxed ride off road. Shift often to maintain a 90-rpm cadence. Light, relaxed pressure on the pedals. Non-technical trail.

E2b   **Rolling hills.** Ride in heart rate Zones 1–2 on a course with small, rolling hills. This can be done on your trainer by shifting gears to simulate small hills.

E2f **Zone 2 ride.** Ride in heart rate Zones 1–2 on a gently rolling course. Get at least 50 percent of your ride time in heart rate Zone 2. Avoid Zones 3–5.

E3b **Seated hills.** Ride in heart rate Zones 2–3, or with power no greater than CP90, on a rolling course. Stay seated on most hills to build leg strength. Spend most of the ride in the aero position.

E3c **Moderate group ride.** Ride mostly in heart rate Zones 1–3 or CP60–180 on a rolling course. This may be a group ride. Avoid Zone 5 or more power than CP30. No hard, sustained pulls. Spend most of the ride sitting in the pack.

E4aL **Racecourse practice.** Ride on a course that mimics your A race. Ride at a steady pace, finishing at the same speed as you started. Start with a low level of perceived exertion and increase gradually throughout the ride to maintain a constant speed. Eat and drink steadily during this ride using exactly the same fueling regime that you plan to use on race day.

E4bL **Aerobic threshold ride.** Ride on a course that mimics your A race. Use the first hour as a warm-up. During the remainder of the ride, alternate 20 minutes in heart rate Zone 2, or 65 percent of CP30, with 10 minutes in Zone 1, or 50 percent of CP30. Eat and drink steadily during this ride, using exactly the same fueling regime that you plan to use on race day.

E4cL **Off-road racecourse practice.** Ride on an off-road course that mimics your A race. Warm up and then ride the course at or slightly above race pace. Eat and drink using exactly the same fueling regime you plan to use on race day.

FORCE WORKOUTS

F1a **Seated short climbs.** Ride in heart rate Zones 1–4, or up to power Zone CP30, on a trainer. Shift up and down through the gears to simulate hills. Spend 2–5 minutes in each gear. Stay seated to build strength.

F1c **Moderate pace long climbs.** Ride in heart rate Zones 2–4 or CP60–CP90 on a hilly course with long climbs (6+ minutes). Avoid heart rate Zone 5 or powers above CP30. Avoid going anaerobic. Do not force the effort on the hills. Hold back on most climbs. Stay seated on most climbs.

F1d **Fast-pace long climbs.** Ride in heart rate Zones 1-5a on a hilly course with long (6+ minutes), steady climbs of 4-6 percent grades. Power should be at CP12 on climbs. Climb mostly seated at 60-70 rpm.

F2a **Ninety-second big gear intervals.** Ride on a trainer adjusted to a high-resistance setting. Do the following 8-12 times: 30 seconds at 70-80 rpm, 30-second shift-up, 30-second shift-up, 90-second recovery. If using power, do 30 seconds at CP60, 30 seconds at CP30, 30 seconds at CP12, and a 90-second recovery spin. Stay seated throughout.

F2b **One- to two-minute big gear climbs.** Ride several 1-2 minute climbs of varying grades with a max heart rate in the 5a Zone or at CP12. Shift to a higher gear than you would normally use for any given climb. Cadence should be 50-60 rpm. Stay seated. Otherwise ride easy.

F2c **Force intervals.** Ride on flat road or on a trainer. Heart rate is not observed. Use the big chainring and a gear that allows only about 50-60 rpm. While in the saddle, drive the pedals down as hard as possible, or at CP1, for 15-20 revolutions of the cranks. Do 6-10 of these, starting a new one every 3-5 minutes after warming up.

F3a **Fast-pace mixed hills.** Ride on a course with long and short hills in all heart rate zones. By the end, 10 percent or more of your time should have been in the 4-5b Zones. Do long climbs in the saddle at CP12. Attack very short hills at CP1. Work hard on climbs.

SPEED SKILLS WORKOUTS

Heart rate should stay low for all speed skills workouts. Your goal is to train correct neural firing patterns. Stop any skills workout when you become fatigued and cannot continue with perfect technique.

S1aL **Isolated leg training.** Ride on a trainer. Warm up for 15 minutes. Pedal for 30 seconds with your left leg only, 30 seconds with your right leg only (rest your opposite leg on a chair), increase rpm by 5 and spin for 1 minute with both legs. This is one set. Do 7–10 sets with 2–3 minutes of recovery between each set. Work to eliminate the dead spot in your pedal stroke. Any clunking sound from your chain indicates a dead spot.

S1b   **Spin-ups.** Ride on a flat road or trainer. Warm up for 15 minutes. Slowly spin up to max rpm over 30 seconds. When you begin to bounce, back off, and then hold it for several seconds. Recover completely and repeat several times. Stay RELAXED!

S1c   **Dominant-leg pedaling.** Ride on a flat road or trainer. Let one leg do 90 percent of the work for one minute, then switch to the opposite leg. Keep heels slightly raised. Focus on a complete pedal stroke; at the top, push the toes forward in the shoe; at the bottom pull back and up as if you are scraping mud off the sole. Maintain low perceived exertion, heart rate, and power output.

S1d   **Dominant-leg spin-ups.** Ride on a flat road or trainer. Warm up for 15 minutes. Do the following three times: 10 seconds at high rpm, 10 seconds higher, 10 seconds max, and then recover for 60 seconds. Then do this three times: 30 seconds of left-leg-dominant pedaling (left leg does 90 percent of the work and other leg loafs) and then 30 seconds of right-leg-dominant pedaling. Repeat the entire sequence 4–5 times. Use your small chainring.

S1e   **Downhill spins.** Ride a rolling course. Instead of coasting downhill, as you gather speed on the descent, increase your leg speed without shifting gears. Pedal as fast as you can to "keep up." When you hear a clunking sound (that occurs when you lose tension on the chain) or start bouncing in the saddle, shift up a gear to "catch up." Stay smooth.

S1eL   **Straight-line downhill spins.** Ride exactly as in workout S1e, but pay particular attention to riding in a straight line. If you are riding along the painted white line at the side of the road, your tires should never leave the line. (Only ride on the white line if you are sure it is safe to do so.)

S1f   **Granny-gear sprints.** On a flat section of road, shift into your smallest gear and pedal smoothly, as fast as you can, for 30 seconds. These can be fun to do with partners.

S3c   **Handling skills.** Work on handling skills in a parking lot. Slalom, pick up water bottles, make tight turns, hop, do track stands, etc.

S6aL   **Off-road ride.** Periodically do a total body inventory from head to toe and check that all nonworking muscles are relaxed. Wiggle your fingers and toes. Check that your elbows are bent and your shoulders are relaxed. Practice pedaling in a relaxed and smooth manner while seated, over bumpy terrain.

S7aL   **Off-road ride.** Continually scan up and down the trail with your vision, but spend most of the time with your eyes focused 6 seconds ahead on the trail. Count the seconds it takes for a tree that is in your focal point to pass your front wheel. Practice at different speeds.

MUSCULAR ENDURANCE WORKOUTS

M1a   **Tempo intervals.** Warm up well on a flat course or trainer. Ride 4–5 x 6 minutes in heart rate Zone 3 or CP90 (2-minute recoveries). Otherwise ride in heart rate Zones 1–2. Focus on smooth pedaling at 90–100 rpm. Stay in the aero position.

M1b   **Tempo.** Warm up well on a flat course or trainer. Ride 20–40 minutes nonstop in heart rate Zone 3 or CP90; otherwise ride in heart rate Zones 1–2. Focus on smooth pedaling at 90–100 rpm. Stay in the aero position.

M1d   **Cruise intervals.** Warm up well on a flat course or trainer. Ride 4–5 x 6 minutes in heart rate Zones 4–5a or CP30 (2-minute recoveries); otherwise ride in heart rate Zones 1–2. Focus on smooth pedaling at 90–100 rpm. Stay in the aero position.

M1e   **Time-trial intervals.** Warm up well on a flat course or trainer on time-trial setup. Ride 3 x 10km building to heart rate Zones 5a–low 5b or CP30–CP12 (5-minute recoveries); otherwise ride in heart rate Zones 1–2. Focus on smooth pedaling at 90–100 rpm. Stay in the aero position.

M1f   **Long tempo.** Warm up well on a flat course or trainer. Ride 40–60 minutes nonstop in heart rate Zone 3 or CP90; otherwise ride in heart rate Zones 1–2. Focus on smooth pedaling at 90–100 rpm. Stay in the aero position.

M1g   Very long tempo. Warm up well on a flat course or trainer. Ride 60–90 minutes nonstop in heart rate Zone 3 or CP90; otherwise ride in heart rate Zones 1–2. Focus on smooth pedaling at 90–100 rpm. Stay in the aero position.

M2b   Hill cruise intervals. Warm up well. Climb a 6- to 8-minute hill (4–6 percent grade) 3–4 times in heart rate Zones 4–5a or CP30. Stay seated. Pedal smoothly at 60–70 rpm.

M2d   Time-trial cruise intervals. Warm up well. On a time trial-bike ride 3–4 x 6–8 minutes up a 2-percent hill (or into a headwind) in heart rate Zones 4–5a or CP30. Focus on smooth pedaling at 90–100 rpm. Stay in the aero position.

M2e   Hill threshold. Warm up well. Ride 20–30 minutes up a steady grade in heart rate Zones 4–5a or CP60. Stay seated. Pedal smoothly at 60–70 rpm.

M3a   Crisscross threshold. Warm up well on a flat course. Ride 20 minutes in heart rate Zones 4–5a or CP60–CP12. Crisscross from low-4 to high-5a Zones or CP60–CP12 every 1–2 minutes. Focus on smooth pedaling at 90–100 rpm. Stay in the aero position.

M3b   Threshold. Warm up well on a flat course. Ride 25–30 minutes nonstop in heart rate Zones 4–5a or CP60. Focus on smooth pedaling at 90–100 rpm. Stay in the aero position.

M3c   Long threshold. Warm up well on a flat course. Ride 50–60 minutes nonstop in the heart rate Zones 3–5a or CP90. Focus on smooth pedaling at 90–100 rpm. Stay in the aero position.

M3dL   Power-pulse ME intervals. Warm up well, then ride at goal CP30 until your heart rate exceeds LTHR + 3bpm. Spin easy for 25 percent of the work-interval time and then repeat three times. Reset your goal CP30 when you have a work interval lasting 20 minutes or more.

M4a   Climbing. On an off-road course, warm up well and then ride 4–6 x 3–5 minutes up a steep hill in heart rate Zones 4–5a or at CP30. Get in about 20 minutes of climbing.

M4bL   Off-road time trial. On an off-road course, warm up well and then time trial for 20 minutes, building to heart rate Zone 4 or CP60. Spin easily for 10 minutes and then repeat 1–2 times.

M5a   **Warm-up rehearsal.** Rehearse the warm-up routine you will use for tomorrow's race. Then get off your legs.

M5bL   **Taper repeats.** After warm up, ride 4 x 90 seconds at race pace (3-minute recoveries). Finish with a very easy cool-down and stretch.

ANAEROBIC ENDURANCE WORKOUTS

A1d   **30/30s.** Warm up very well on a flat course. Ride 15–20 x 30 seconds at 90 percent effort (9 on 1–10 RPE scale) or CP6 with 30-second, easy spin recoveries. Stop if speed drops by 1 mph or power drops below CP6. Use a rolling start for each repeat. Get to the top end quickly.

A2a   **Time-trial intervals.** Warm up very well on a flat course. Ride 5 x 5km (5-minute recoveries) building to heart rate Zones 5a–5b or CP12. Increase gear size for the first three repeats. Focus on smooth pedaling at 90–100 rpm. Stay in the aero position.

A2aL   **Three-minute flat intervals.** Warm up very well on a flat course. Ride 5 x 3 minutes (3-minutes recoveries) building to heart rate Zones 5a–b or CP12. Focus on smooth pedaling at 90–100 rpm.

A2b   **Three-minute hill intervals.** Warm up very well. Ride up a 6–8 pre cent hill 4–5 x 3 minutes in heart rate Zone 5b or CP6 (3-minute recoveries). Stay seated and pedal at a cadence of 70+ rpm.

A2d   **Three-minute hill intervals and threshold.** Warm up very well. Ride up a 4–6 percent hill 4–5 x 3 minutes to the heart rate Zone 5b or CP6 (3-minute recoveries). Stay seated on each and pedal at a cadence of 60–70 rpm. Then ride 20 minutes in heart rate Zones 4–5a or CP60 on a mostly flat course. Focus on smooth pedaling at 90–100 rpm. Stay in the aero position.

A2e   **Three-minute moderate hill intervals.** Warm up very well. Ride up a 2 percent hill or into a headwind 4–5 x 3 minutes to the heart rate Zone 5b or CP6 (3-minute recoveries). Focus on smooth pedaling at 90–100 rpm. Stay in the aero position.

A3c   **Ninety-second hill intervals.** Warm up very well. Ride up a 6–8 percent hill 4–5 x 90 seconds. The first 60 seconds of each is seated at 60+ rpm. Stand for the last 30 seconds. Achieve heart rate Zone 5c by the top, or ride in CP6 while seated and CP1 while standing. (Recover 3 minutes after each.)

A3d   **Ninety-second hill intervals and threshold.** Warm up very well. Ride up a 6-8 percent hill 4-5 x 90 seconds. Stay seated for the first 60 seconds of each, then stand for the last 30 seconds of each. Achieve the heart rate 5c Zone by the top, or ride in CP6 while seated and CP1 while standing. (Recover 3 minutes after each.) Then ride 20 minutes in the heart rate Zones 4-5a or CP60 on a mostly flat course. Focus on smooth pedaling at 90-100 rpm. Stay in the aero position.

POWER WORKOUTS

Heart rate is not a measure you can use to guide your exercise intensity in power workouts due to the short duration of the efforts and the time lag in the heart rate response to exercise. Power measurement in watts with a power meter is a direct and immediate measure of exercise intensity and is the best measure to use to guide power workouts.

P1c   **Short sprints.** Warm up well. On varying terrain, ride three sets of 5 x 8-12 second sprints at CP0.2 or max effort with 3 minutes of recovery between sprints and 5 minutes of recovery between sets.

P1d   **Long sprints.** Warm up well. Every 5 minutes select a BIG gear and ride at CP1; stand for 10 seconds, sit for 10 seconds. Pedal smoothly at a cadence of 100+ rpm. Stop when your power drops 5 percent.

P2a   **Short hill sprints.** Warm up well. Ride up a 3-5 percent hill with 5-7 x 8-12 second sprints at CP0.2 or max effort, with 3 minutes of recovery between sprints. Sit and stand. Pedal smoothly at a cadence of 90+ rpm.

P2b   **Long hill sprints.** Warm up well. Ride three sets up a 3-5 percent hill of 3 x 15-20 second sprints at CP1, with 3 minutes of recovery between sprints and 5 minutes of recovery between sets. Sit and stand. Pedal smoothly at a cadence of 90+ rpm.

Annual Training Plan Worksheet

Athlete_____

Annual Hours (See Chapter 10 for guidelines to set annual hours.)
Season Goals (See Chapter 8 for goal-setting guidelines.)

1. _____

2. _____

3. _____

Preparation Period
Period Objectives (See Chapter 9 for objective setting guidelines.)

1. _____

2. _____

3. _____

4. _____

5. _____

WEEK	HOURS*	MON.	TUES.	WED.	THURS.	FRI.	SAT.	SUN.
1								
2								
3								
4								

*See Table 10.1

Base 1 Period
Period Objectives

1. _____

2. _____

3. _____

4. _____

5. _____

WEEK	HOURS*	MON.	TUES.	WED.	THURS.	FRI.	SAT.	SUN.
1								
2								
3								
4								

*See Table 10.1

Base 2 Period
Period Objectives

1. _____

2. _____

3. _____

4. _____

5. _____

WEEK	HOURS*	MON.	TUES.	WED.	THURS.	FRI.	SAT.	SUN.
1								
2								
3								
4								

*See Table 10.1

Base 3 Period
Period Objectives

1. _____

2. _____

3. _____

4. _____

5. _____

WEEK	HOURS*	MON.	TUES.	WED.	THURS.	FRI.	SAT.	SUN.
1								
2								
3								
4								

*See Table 10.1

Build 1 Period
Period Objectives

1. _____

2. _____

3. _____

4. _____

5. _____

WEEK	HOURS*	MON.	TUES.	WED.	THURS.	FRI.	SAT.	SUN.
1								
2								
3								
4								

*See Table 10.1

Build 2 Period
Period Objectives

1. _____

2. _____

3. _____

4. _____

5. _____

WEEK	HOURS*	MON.	TUES.	WED.	THURS.	FRI.	SAT.	SUN.
1								
2								
3								
4								

*See Table 10.1

Peak Period
Period Objectives

1. _____

2. _____

3. _____

4. _____

5. _____

WEEK	HOURS*	MON.	TUES.	WED.	THURS.	FRI.	SAT.	SUN.
1								
2								

*See Table 10.1

Race Period
Period Objectives

1. _____

2. _____

3. _____

4. _____

5. _____

WEEK	HOURS*	MON.	TUES.	WED.	THURS.	FRI.	SAT.	SUN.
1								

*See Table 10.1

Transition Period
Period Objectives

1. _____

2. _____

3. _____

4. _____

5. _____

WEEK	HOURS*	MON.	TUES.	WED.	THURS.	FRI.	SAT.	SUN.
1								
2								
3								
4								

*See Table 10.1

Training Journal

WEEK BEGINNING: TRAINING PERIOD:

Training period objectives (check off as achieved)

- 1. _____
- 2. _____
- 3. _____
- 4. _____
- 5. _____

MONDAY / /	TUESDAY / /

Sleep ▢ Fatigue ▢ Stress ▢ Soreness | Sleep ▢ Fatigue ▢ Stress ▢ Soreness

Resting heart rate _____ Weight _____ | Resting heart rate _____ Weight _____

Workout 1

S   B   R   O _____

Duration _____ Weather _____

Route _____

_____

Distance _____ Time _____

Time
by zone   1   2   3   4   5

Workout rating _____

Notes _____

_____

Workout 2

S   B   R   O _____

Duration _____ Weather _____

Route _____

_____

Distance _____ Time _____

Time
by zone   1   2   3   4   5

Workout rating _____

Notes _____

_____

Workout 1

S   B   R   O _____

Duration _____ Weather _____

Route _____

_____

Distance _____ Time _____

Time
by zone   1   2   3   4   5

Workout rating _____

Notes _____

_____

Workout 2

S   B   R   O _____

Duration _____ Weather _____

Route _____

_____

Distance _____ Time _____

Time
by zone   1   2   3   4   5

Workout rating _____

Notes _____

_____

| **WEDNESDAY** | / | / | **THURSDAY** | / | / |

□ Sleep □ Fatigue □ Stress □ Soreness

Resting heart rate _____ Weight _____

Workout 1
S   B   R   O _____

Duration _____ Weather _____

Route _____

_____

_____

Distance _____ Time _____

Time
by zone **1   2   3   4   5**

Workout rating _____

Notes _____

_____

_____

_____

Workout 2
S   B   R   O _____

Duration _____ Weather _____

Route _____

_____

_____

Distance _____ Time _____

Time
by zone **1   2   3   4   5**

Workout rating _____

Notes _____

_____

_____

□ Sleep □ Fatigue □ Stress □ Soreness

Resting heart rate _____ Weight _____

Workout 1
S   B   R   O _____

Duration _____ Weather _____

Route _____

_____

_____

Distance _____ Time _____

Time
by zone **1   2   3   4   5**

Workout rating _____

Notes _____

_____

_____

_____

Workout 2
S   B   R   O _____

Duration _____ Weather _____

Route _____

_____

_____

Distance _____ Time _____

Time
by zone **1   2   3   4   5**

Workout rating _____

Notes _____

_____

_____

FRIDAY   /   /

Sleep   Fatigue   Stress   Soreness

Resting heart rate _____ Weight _____

Workout 1
S   B   R   O _____

Duration _____ Weather _____

Route _____

_____

_____

Distance _____ Time _____
Time
by zone 1   2   3   4   5

Workout rating _____

Notes _____

_____

_____

Workout 2
S   B   R   O _____

Duration _____ Weather _____

Route _____

_____

_____

Distance _____ Time _____
Time
by zone 1   2   3   4   5

Workout rating _____

Notes _____

_____

_____

SATURDAY   /   /

Sleep   Fatigue   Stress   Soreness

Resting heart rate _____ Weight _____

Workout 1
S   B   R   O _____

Duration _____ Weather _____

Route _____

_____

_____

Distance _____ Time _____
Time
by zone 1   2   3   4   5

Workout rating _____

Notes _____

_____

_____

Workout 2
S   B   R   O _____

Duration _____ Weather _____

Route _____

_____

_____

Distance _____ Time _____
Time
by zone 1   2   3   4   5

Workout rating _____

Notes _____

_____

_____

SUNDAY	/	/

■ Sleep   ■ Fatigue   ■ Stress   ■ Soreness

Resting heart rate _____   Weight _____

Workout 1

S   B   R   O _____

Duration _____   Weather _____

Route _____

_____

_____

Distance _____   Time _____

Time
by zone   **1   2   3   4   5**

Workout rating _____

Notes _____

_____

_____

Workout 2

S   B   R   O _____

Duration _____   Weather _____

Route _____

_____

_____

Distance _____   Time _____

Time
by zone   **1   2   3   4   5**

Workout rating _____

Notes _____

_____

_____

_____

RACE: _____

	Distance	Time	Place (overall/division)
Swim			
Tran 1	—		
Bike			
Tran 2	—		
Run			
Finish	—		

Notes _____

_____

_____

_____

_____

WEEKLY SUMMARY

	Time/dist.	Year to date
Swim		
Bike		
Run		
Strength		

Weekly total _____   Year-to-date total _____

Soreness _____

Notes _____

_____

_____

Test Results Worksheet

TEST RESULTS WORKSHEET

30-minute time trial, maximum effort

Date _____

Athlete _____

Waking body weight _____

Waking resting heart rate _____

Time of test _____

Time of last food intake before test _____

Equipment used _____

Warm-up protocol _____

Test course description _____

_____

Temp _____ Humidity _____ Wind conditions _____

Notes _____

_____

Exact distance covered in 30 minutes _____

Average speed for 30 minutes _____

Maximum speed observed during test _____

Average heart rate for final 20 minutes for time trial _____

Maximum heart rate observed during test _____

Average power for 30 minutes (watts) _____

Maximum power observed during test _____

Average cadence observed during test _____

Maximum cadence observed during test _____

Perceived exertion at end of test (1–10) _____

Glossary

Adaptation. Refers to the body's ability to adjust to various demands placed on it over a period of time.

Aerobic capacity. The body's maximal capacity for using oxygen to produce energy during maximal exertion. Also known as VO_2 max.

Aerobic. In the presence of oxygen; aerobic metabolism utilizes oxygen. Below the anaerobic-intensity level.

Agonistic muscles. Muscles directly engaged in a muscular contraction.

Anaerobic threshold (AT). When aerobic metabolism no longer supplies all the need for energy, energy is produced anaerobically; indicated by an increase in lactic acid. Sometimes referred to as lactate threshold.

Anaerobic-endurance. The ability resulting from the combination of speed skills and endurance allowing the athlete to maintain a high speed for an extended period of time while anaerobic.

Anaerobic. Literally "without oxygen." Exercise that demands more oxygen than the heart and lungs can supply. The intensity of exercise performed above the lactate threshold.

Base period. The period during which the basic abilities of endurance, speed skills, and strength are emphasized.

Bonk. A state of extreme exhaustion mainly caused by the depletion of glycogen in the muscles.

Build period. The specific preparation mesocycle during which high-intensity training in the form of muscular-endurance, speed-endurance, and power are emphasized, and endurance, force, and speed skills are maintained.

Cadence. Revolutions or cycles per minute of the pedal stroke.

Capillary. A small vessel located between arteries and veins in which exchanges between tissue and blood occur.

Cardiorespiratory system. Cardiovascular system and lungs.

Cardiovascular system. Heart, blood, and blood vessels.

Central nervous system. Spinal cord and brain.

Cool-down. Low-intensity exercise at the end of a training session.

Cross-training. Training for more than one sport during the same period of time.

Drafting. Cycling behind others in order to reduce effort.

Drops. The lower portion of turned-down handlebars.

Duration. The length of time of a given workout.

Endurance. The ability to persist, to resist fatigue.

Ergogenic aid. A substance, device, or phenomenon that can improve athletic performance.

Fartlek. Swedish for "speed play," or an unstructured, interval-type workout.

Fast-twitch fiber (FT). A muscle fiber characterized by fast contraction time, high anaerobic capacity, and low aerobic capacity, all making the fiber suited for high-power activities.

Force. The strength evident in a muscle or muscle group while exerting against a resistance.

Frequency. The number of times per week that one trains.

Glucose. A simple sugar.

Glycemic index. A system of ranking carbohydrate foods based on how quickly they raise the blood's glucose level.

Glycogen. The form in which glucose (sugar) is stored in the muscles and the liver.

Growth hormone. A hormone secreted by the anterior lobe of the pituitary gland that stimulates growth and development.

Hammer. A fast, sustained effort.

Hamstring. Muscle on the back of the thigh that flexes the knee and extends the hip.

Hoods. On drop handlebars, the covers of the brake handles.

Individuality, principle of. The theory that any training program must consider the specific needs and abilities of the individual for whom it is designed.

Intensity. The qualitative element of training referring to effort, velocity, maximum strength, and power.

Interval training. A system of high-intensity work marked by short, but regularly repeated periods of hard exercise interspersed with periods of recovery.

Isolated leg training (ILT). Pedaling with one leg to improve technique.

Lactate threshold (LT). The point during exercise of increasing intensity at which blood lactate begins to accumulate above resting levels. Sometimes referred to as anaerobic threshold.

Lactate. Formed when lactic acid from the muscles enters the bloodstream.

Lactic acid. A by-product of the lactic acid system resulting from the incomplete breakdown of glucose (sugar) in the production of energy.

Mash. To push a big gear.

Mesocycle. A period of training generally two to six weeks long.

Microcycle. A period of training of approximately one week.

Muscular endurance. The ability of a muscle or muscle group to perform repeated contractions for a long period of time while bearing a load.

Overload, principle of. A training load that challenges the body's current level of fitness.

Overreaching. Training above the workload that would produce overtraining if continued long enough.

Overtraining. Extreme fatigue, both physical and mental, caused by extensively training at a workload higher than that to which the body can readily adapt.

Peak period. The mesocycle during which volume of training is reduced and intensity is proportionally increased allowing the athlete to reach high levels of fitness.

Periodization. The process of structuring training into periods.

Power. The ability resulting from force and speed skills.

Preparation (Prep) period. The mesocycle during which the athlete begins to train for the coming season; usually marked by the use of cross-training and low workloads.

Progression, principle of. The theory that the workload must be gradually increased accompanied by intermittent periods of recovery.

Quadriceps. The large muscle in front of the thigh that extends the lower leg and flexes the hip.

Race period. The mesocycle during which the workload is greatly decreased allowing the athlete to compete in high-priority races.

Rating of perceived exertion (RPE). A subjective assessment of how hard one is working.

Recovery interval. The relief period between work intervals within an interval workout.

Recovery. A period of training when rest is emphasized.

Repetition. The number of times a task, such as a work interval or lifting of a weight, is repeated.

Session. A single practice period that may include one or more workouts.

Set. A group of repetitions.

Single leg pedaling. Pedaling technique drill using one leg at a time (see also isolated leg training).

Slow-twitch fiber (ST). A muscle fiber characterized by slow contraction time, low anaerobic capacity, and high aerobic capacity, all making the fiber suited for low power, long-duration activities.

Specificity, principle of. The theory that training must stress the systems critical for optimal performance in order to achieve the desired training adaptations.

Speed skills. Within the context of this book, the ability to move the body in ways that produce optimum performance. For example, the ability to turn the cranks quickly and efficiently on the bike.

Singletrack. A trail wide enough only for one rider.

Spin. To pedal lightly in an easy gear.

Tactic. Anything you can do to help yourself get ahead of your opponents.

Tapering. A reduction in training volume prior to a major competition.

Tops. The portion of the handlebar closest to the stem.

Training zone. A level of intensity based on a percentage of some measure, such as heart rate or power, of the individual's capacity for work.

Training. A comprehensive program intended to prepare an athlete for competition.

Transition (Tran) period. The mesocycle during which the workload and structure of training are greatly reduced, allowing physical and psychological recovery from training and racing.

Ventilatory threshold (VT). The point during increasing exertion at which breathing first becomes labored. Closely corresponds with lactate threshold.

VO₂max. The capacity for oxygen consumption by the body during maximal exertion, also known as aerobic capacity and maximal oxygen consumption. Usually expressed as liters of oxygen consumed per kilogram of body weight per minute (ml/kg/min).

Volume. A quantitative element of training, such as miles or hours of training within a given time. The combination of duration and frequency.

Warm-up. The period of gradually increasing intensity of exercise at the start of a training session.

Work interval. High intensity efforts separated by recovery intervals.

Workload. Measured stress applied in training through the combination of frequency, intensity, and duration.

Workout. A portion of a session that is focused on a specific aspect of training, such as power.

Xterra. Brand name for popular off-road triathlon series.

Index

Letters appearing after page numbers denote the following:
p = photo; f = figure; t = table.

About the Author

Lynda Wallenfels is an elite-level USA Cycling coach, Level II USA Triathlon coach, and an Ultrafit Associate. Her clients boast top ten finishes at ironman-distance and Xterra events. An accomplished athlete herself, Lynda has raced as a professional cyclist since 1994, with two years on the British National Team and three national championship titles. In 1999 she became an American citizen and won the 2004 U.S. 100-mile mountain bike national championships. Lynda expresses her passion for triathlon and cycling as a regular contributor to *VeloNews*, *Inside Triathlon*, Active.com, Ultrafit e-tips, and her Web site www.LWCoaching.com. She makes her home in the red rock desert of Southern Utah, where she lives with her husband Steve and their children Emma and Wesley.

Lynda always enjoys discussing training and racing on her Web site discussion forum, http://www.lwcoaching.com/forum/index.php. She is available for coaching and consulting and can be contacted through her Web site or at Lynda@LWCoaching.com.